MW00468844

What Are People Saying about

Is He Nuts?

"Dennis is one of the finest men I know. We've become friends since he became a Latter-day Saint. Dennis has helped me to better understand God's LGBTQ children and the gifts and Christlike attributes they bring to the body of Christ and how we need people like Dennis in our congregations to help us better come unto Christ. I encourage every religion to read Dennis's book to better understand God's LGBTQ children on how they are not a separate people or community, but rather fellow children of a loving God."

> ~ Richard Ostler, former YSA Bishop, Salt Lake City, UT,
> www.listenlearnandlove.org

"Dennis Schleicher shares his compelling faith-filled journey as a gay man joining The Church of Jesus Christ of Latter-day Saints at a time when so many LGBTQ were leaving the Church. As an active Latter-day Saint mother of an openly gay son, I was moved by Dennis's story and the pure love of Christ. A must-read for all who are seeking to walk in the shoes of another."

> ~ Becky Mackintosh, Lehi, Utah. Her story is featured on our
> official website: mormonandgay.lds.org/stories

"I love what Dennis has done here. In sharing his story, he has bared his soul to the Church and the world—something I wish we would all do more frequently as members of the Church. Being honest and authentic about who we are and the challenges we face allows the Spirit to be more fully present and allows us to more fully bear one another's burdens. By being vulnerable in this way, Dennis invites us to feel what it might be like to be in his position as a gay man who must grapple with the challenge of finding a faith he calls home but that is still learning how to love and incorporate its gay members. Are we willing to bear the burdens of our fellow LGBT members of the Church and make a place for them among us? Reading this book will help us start on that path."

~ Bryce Cook, active member, father
of six kids (two of whom are gay)

"An individual's search for the divine is a special experience that shouldn't be denied anyone. In a world where queer folks are often rejected by their faith communities, we need to hear more stories of queer folks of faith, and Dennis provides one of those much-needed stories. As a person who has often felt too gay for the Mormons and too Mormon for the gays, I commend Dennis for finding his place and having the courage to share his story."

~ Peter Moosman, #HugAGayMormon

"Dennis is one of the most amazing and wonderful people I had the privilege to meet as I served as a missionary for The Church of Jesus Christ of Latter-day Saints in the Massachusetts, Connecticut, and Rhode Island area. One of the things I love the most about Dennis is his willingness to share his story with others and his big heart. Before meeting him, I was naive in my knowledge and thoughts on the LGBT community. Since I had never met a member of the Church that was from LGBT community, I had never looked into the Church's beliefs, or even my own, on this topic. I am truly grateful for Dennis and his influence in my life, which allowed me to open my eyes and see things in a different way."

~ Sister Kaylie Sorensen, São Paulo, Brazil, returned missionary
for The Church of Jesus Christ of Latter-day Saints

"No matter what religion, faith background, sexual orientation, or race you have or are, I challenge you to choose love! Open your heart and it will clear your mind. Loving and accepting all is a true Christlike attribute. This is also what I've learned and have chosen to do as an openly gay Mormon. I couldn't be more proud of my friend Dennis for sharing his experiences and story. Creating a safe space for LGBTQ Mormons is something I'm equally as passionate about. It gives me hope for the future of LGBTQ Mormons when I see individuals like Dennis who are being vulnerable by speaking their truth, bringing to light the gospel of Jesus Christ, and building the kingdom of God, where inclusivity is a must. Thank you, Dennis, for your courage and for your mission."

~ Jena Lowry Peterson, openly gay Mormon,
life coach and speaker

"Dennis's words prompt me to learn more about the LGBT community. I want to listen, learn, and LOVE more deliberately as an open-minded disciple of Christ. How may I be a blessing to my brothers and sisters who bear the burden of being misunderstood by even well-meaning people? The Lord gradually removed spiritual cataracts from your eyes to allow you to see and feel the love of Christ through His true disciples. We ALL need to know we are LOVED just as we are! You searched for and found the truth because you were ready to act upon it through baptism and attending the temple. Others are also ready to hear Lord's the plan of salvation. Your story will open and heal hearts and families."

"I want to help you #TurnUpTheLove and am willing to help anytime and anywhere.

"I stand with you to protect and defend those who are maligned.

"I will openly share messages about the gospel of Jesus Christ."

~ Elizabeth Saede, Stoninington, Connecticut, author and
convert into The Church of Jesus Christ of Latter-day Saints

Is He Nuts?

Why a Gay Man Would Become a
Member of the Church of Jesus Christ

Dennis Schleicher

CFI

An imprint of Cedar Fort, Inc.
Springville, Utah

ISBN 13: 978-1-4621-3571-4

Published by CFI, an imprint of Cedar Fort, Inc.
2373 W. 700 S., Springville, UT 84663
Distributed by Cedar Fort, Inc., www.cedarfort.com

LIBRARY OF CONGRESS CATALOGING-IN-PUBLICATION DATA

Names: Schleicher, Dennis, 1972- author.
Title: Is he nuts? : why a gay man would become a member of the Church of
   Jesus Christ / Dennis Schleicher.
Description: Springville, Utah : CFI, an imprint of Cedar Fort, Inc., [2019]
   | Includes bibliographical references.
Identifiers: LCCN 2019002064 (print) | LCCN 2019003476 (ebook) | ISBN
   9781462131037 (epub, pdf, mobi) | ISBN 9781462135714 (perfect bound : alk.
   paper)
Subjects: LCSH: Schleicher, Dennis, 1972- | Mormon gays. | Mormon converts.
Classification: LCC BX8643.H65 (ebook) | LCC BX8643.H65 S35 2019 (print) |
   DDC 289.3086/64--dc23
LC record available at https://lccn.loc.gov/2019002064

Cover design by Jeff Harvey
Cover design © 2019 Cedar Fort, Inc.
Edited by Trina Caudle, Kathryn Watkins, and Kaitlin Barwick
Typeset by Kaitlin Barwick

Printed in the United States of America

10 9 8 7 6 5 4 3 2 1

Printed on acid-free paper

This is dedicated to all of the children and adults who have taken their own lives due to a sexual identity crisis. My heart goes out to their families and friends as I pray and ponder daily, hoping that they will feel the presence of the Holy Ghost. I pray that they will receive comfort and peace by continuing to believe in the restored gospel.

This is also dedicated to my younger brother, Darin Scott Schleicher, my best friend and the most supportive in my family regarding my sexuality. I was so honored and privileged to perform your ordinances in the temple—it will always be remembered, and I will return to our Heavenly Father and you with honor.

Contents

Foreword by Al Carraway x

Prologue xiv

Chapter 1: The Punishment for Confusion 1

Chapter 2: A Study in Contradictions 8

Chapter 3: O Beloved Brother 22

Chapter 4: Looking for Love 38

Chapter 5: Reset Button on Life 48

Chapter 6: They're Nuts. I Don't Want to Go to Palmyra! 59

Chapter 7: Meet the Mormons 74

Chapter 8: Two Steps Forward, One Step Back 81

Chapter 9: The Plunge 100

Chapter 10: The Wind beneath My Wings 110

Chapter 11: Opposition in All Things 119

Chapter 12: Called to Serve 123

Chapter 13: I'm Out 133

Chapter 14: Temple Time 138

Chapter 15: Why I Believe 148

Chapter 16: Walking in Sunlight 152

Resources 157

References 158

Acknowledgments 159

About the Author 161

Foreword

by Al Carraway

Author of *More than the Tattooed Mormon*
and *Wildly Optimistic*

I don't fit the mold for anything. I don't fit the mold of how I look in my religion or my community, or what I'm trying to tackle and talk about and pursue. How can someone succeed when everything about them in their demographic implies that they shouldn't? It's like I was failing before I could even start. Sometimes fears are just in our head and we imagine the worst-case scenario, and that's enough to stop before starting. But not in my case; mine was a reality. I couldn't go anywhere or post anything without those terrible stares, mean comments, rude remarks, assumptions of my hatred toward the gospel and toward God, emails saying I should end my life or that God could never love someone like me. It was a long time of loneliness and heartache and weight and judging and confusion and anger—anger toward others, toward myself, and also toward God. *How could they act like this? Maybe they're right. Maybe I'm flawed and just not good enough. Maybe it's not worth it.*

But then I just got tired, you know? Tired of feeling down all the time. Tired of noticing and hearing all this negativity. Tired of not being myself. Tired of having other people tell me how my life should be. I don't have time to let other people's experiences and advice dictate my decisions. We're only living this mortality thing once, and we shouldn't let someone else pick for us.

It was a lot of soul searching and soul stretching. It really was deep loneliness, painful sacrifice, and loss. I've never known real pain until then. Indescribable anguish. I've never struggled so long and so hard where my body would literally ache before, until I got baptized. Times where I felt like I was being punished, times I felt overlooked, unimportant, forgotten.

You're not alone in your wonderings. Like you, I also know what it is to wonder, to doubt, to struggle, to sink, to feel empty, judged, abandoned, unwanted, unworthy, tired, tried, alone, out of sight, unnamed, and unimportant. Like you, I know how hard it is, losing our voice, losing hope, losing strength. Wondering where our place is. Forcing ourselves to use faith we don't even know if we have or not.

What if we got it all backward? What if all of this, all of our hard and unexpected, isn't for us to wonder and doubt, isn't meant to move us backward and slow us down? What if it's bringing us to something different? Something better?

Sometimes all I felt I had was this supposed God and a hope that what I was taught wasn't in vain. But because of it all, I know Him. Because of it all, *I know* God. And I love Him with a real love. And I couldn't trade that knowledge and relationship for anything. Because of it all, I've accomplished and embraced and tried and created and overcome and become because of merging my life with God. Because of it all, I am living a life I didn't even know was available for myself. A better one.

Every time that I wondered where God was and if He really cared about me—each of those moments has brought me to every-thing I have now. It was every single time I was pleading for things to be over and for things to be different that has brought me to every single thing I have now, and it breaks my heart to imagine my life any different. And through it all, I have found *me*. The real me. Who I was meant to be all along, and *oh, what a feeling!* And I dedicate myself to living a life I am excited about and I am proud of. I dedi-cate myself to my wanderings and my wonderings and my sacrifices, and to the unexpected paths God has brought me down because I decided I was going to stop keeping God at arm's length. I decided I was going to allow myself to give God the opportunity to show me how great He really is.

It was a lot of pushing my comfort levels and a whole lot of tearing down to undo and rebuild. It was a lot of honest conversations with my Creator. I desperately needed to see myself how God saw me—even a sliver, because I wasn't seeing it. But our efforts and our faith are never in vain. I have come to know that we see our differences as weaknesses or a setbacks, but what so many fail to recognize is that those aspects that make us different are what we need to *grow* in. It's our individual differences that make progress, success, and change for the better. If we were all the same, how stupid would that be? We as humankind literally wouldn't get anything done.

Being a completely tattooed public speaker for The Church of Jesus Christ might seem ironic and impossible, but I'm doing it. I create. I write. I speak. I progress. I grow. I conquer. I win. I surprise. And I make things happen because I have never told myself I couldn't—and most definitely, I have never been told that I couldn't by my God. Because it is exactly my differences that have brought me to everything I have and am doing now. It is everything that makes me different that has made me help others and succeed into something far bigger than I ever could have imagined. What could our life look like when we give it all to God and trust, especially trust in the discomfort?

When we hear that God is an unchanging God, we think that means His commandments are just unchanging. But that also means His love. His love for us is unchanging, never weakening, always there. And knowing that our God is unchanging means that our helping God will always be a helping God. That our God will always be a God of miracles. Of mercy. Of guidance. Of revelation. Our unchanging God means that His love for His children is also unchanging. Our God will always be a loving God that is bound to His promises to us if we are trying in any degree.

Beautifully written with great passion and honesty and humor, Dennis's story will bring you along for his journey to the reality of experiencing miracles and blessings and opportunities when we allow God to show us how great He really is. Dennis will show you how to embrace who you are and where you are, to embrace the unexpected knowing Who is guiding us and Who is loving us. This book will show us just how life can *blossom* to us when we hold on to the reality that *this is all true.* That God really does live. That Christ really did die and live for *you.* We really are Theirs. God loves us because we are *His.* And that alone makes us enough. Worthy. And Their whole existence is to bring us to the *greater* things.

I do know that God loves me and I am His son whom
He accepts without reservation. My faith in this one
thing is what lifts me above the emotional storm clouds
and helps me to soar through life. I have confidence.

~ Dennis Schleicher

Prologue

July 4th weekend, 1992, Provincetown, Massachusetts. I was surrounded by thousands of gay men wearing everything from miniskirts and heavy makeup to business-casual polos and khaki shorts. My best friend Steven and I were part of the polo-and-khaki crowd, and I had my fake ID tucked into my back pocket because I was only nineteen. The place was packed with men dancing to some of the loudest disco music I've ever experienced, my eardrums vibrating as much as the floor. Everyone was well on their way to being drunk. I stood in a corner of the bar with a drink clenched my hand and twirling the straw as I watched the free-for-all before me.

There has to be more to life than this. What am I doing here?

I'd been told for years that God didn't want me and I was going to hell for being gay. I was supposed to change my whole persona: transform my inner inclinations and become straight, marry a woman, and have children with her. Easier said than done. I didn't choose to be gay. How was I supposed to choose to be straight?

My parents and their evangelical pastors had shouted and screamed at me about hellfire and damnation so much that I refused to go to any church at all. When I was a little boy, I had been the one asking to go to church, and now I had gone in the opposite direction. Even if a church community said that they accepted gays, organized religion left such a bad taste in my mouth that I avoided it entirely.

But I still wondered about faith and life, even in the middle of Provincetown, and I still felt a spiritual pull toward religion. I just didn't have the courage to do anything about it. Yet.

Chapter 1

The Punishment for Confusion

We need more kindness, more compassion, more joy,
more laughter. I definitely want to contribute to that.[1]

~ Ellen DeGeneres

I grew up with a Congregational church literally in my backyard. The summer view out the kitchen window began with my grandfather's tall, bright-yellow sunflowers. The rusty-red brick of the church rose behind them, topped by a stereotypical New England white cupola and a thin, metallic steeple piercing the clear sky. The white-framed windows were opened wide on Sundays, and the music of the hymns floated across the grass to my home.

Our neighborhood cul-de-sac had been built on land owned by my great-grandparents, so we were surrounded by family. My grandparents lived in the house on the left, my great-aunt and uncle on the right. The church parking lot bordered my backyard and was a great place to ride my bike. It was a self-contained, peaceful little world.

We never attended church when I was small, even though it would take less than a minute to get from one door to the other. I was in second grade when I pointed out the window at the steeple and asked my parents, "Why don't we go to church?" My friend Katie went to church there, and I thought it would be fun to have more time with her.

The following Sunday, we walked out the back door, across the yard, and into the church building. Our family was immediately involved in the congregation, attending all of the suppers, fundraisers, picnics, and other events. My mother even held a key to open the church for special occasions and extra meetings.

I was content. I loved the camaraderie and fellowship that occurred on Sundays. My family easily made friends with other families, and I got to see Katie a lot as we attended the children's Sunday School together. I learned about how kind Jesus was and how He wanted us to be kind to others. This was the basis of the good Christian values that would go on to form the bedrock of my life, though I didn't necessarily know it at the time.

However, it seemed that we were only Christians on Sunday mornings during church services and when we had Sunday dinner with our extended family. On Monday morning, everything went back to the usual.

"The usual" was physical abuse from my mother. She suffered from postpartum depression after having me, but "the baby blues" were not properly diagnosed then. It was just something that happened and had to be dealt with by the sufferer alone. From my earliest memories, I associated my mother with pain. Since I didn't know anything else, I thought it was normal, until my younger brother, Darin, was born shortly after I turned four. My mother never laid a hand on him. Much later during therapy, my mother revealed to our counselor and me that she did not want to mess up his life as she had mine.

One evening, my father came into my bedroom and took three teddy bears off my bed. "This is Papa Bear, this is Mama Bear, and this is Baby Bear. What does Mama Bear do when Papa Bear leaves the house?" I smashed the Mama Bear against the Baby Bear. He assured me that he was going to make everything right, but that never amounted to much. He was never home when incidents occurred, so there wasn't much he could do.

About a year after we started attending church, I was playing in the back parking lot with Katie when my mother started screaming for me to return home. I knew what was about to happen and dreaded it, but I had no way to avoid it. I was going to be hit, slapped, and screamed at for no obvious reason. When I came in the door, she grabbed me around my neck and started to jerk me up and down, lifting my feet off the floor. Her hands squeezed together on my trachea, stopping me from breathing. I gasped for air, desperately trying to scream, but no sound could slip through her fingers. All I could do was scream in my head, *Mommy, I can't breathe. You're choking me!*

But I wasn't as small as I used to be. I had grown enough that I was able to break away and run to my bedroom, still having difficulty breathing. It felt like her hands were still around my neck. I could still feel the squeezing and how scary it had been trying to get a breath but not being able to.

My mother was overcome with guilt and locked herself in her bedroom. I was still too terrified to leave my room, but I could hear her crying and moaning for forgiveness, and she called 911. My grandparents heard the sirens and immediately came to our rescue. My grandfather was able to convince my mother to come out and talk to the police. She was sequestered in the living room, and I overheard her telling the police that she had a problem—she couldn't control herself and stop abusing her son. My grandfather contacted my father at work, and within an hour he was home. That evening, my grandparents kept my brother and me at their house, providing comfort in their safe haven as they often did when they could hear my mother screaming from next door.

The next Monday morning, my mother admitted herself into the psychiatric ward at the local hospital. She was there for three weeks and underwent electroshock therapy. Because of its debilitating side effects and arguable benefits, it is now used only as a last resort, but at that time it was a highly recommended treatment.

When I arrived at school that same day, I was called out of class by two social workers from the Department of Family Services. They asked me so many questions that it took me hours to answer them all. But after all of those hours, I never saw them again and nothing came of their endless questions or my honest answers. The early '80s was a completely different time.

For those three weeks of our mom's hospital stay, my brother and I stayed with our grandparents. I had always felt safe there with them, and our grandmother made sure that our school lunches were packed and we maintained our usual routine as much as possible. I'm Gramps's firstborn grandson; I was always a "grandpa's boy." Memories of riding in his truck going on our way to his construction sites always provided a feeling of joy. He taught me a lot about being responsible through demonstrating his hard-work ethics through managing his contracting business. I always marveled at the fact that *my* grandfather could take a wooded field and turn it into a beautiful middle-class neighborhood. I loved going to the construction sites with my grandpa, and I will always cherish the memories from those weeks they took us in.

After my mother returned home, she approached our church's pastor and shared our situation with him. She mentioned to him that she had lost her father when she was a toddler and that perhaps growing up in a single-parent home had affected her emotional state. He recommended that she join a support group held weekly called "Friends of Shanti." It was not part of the church services, but the group had permission to conduct their meetings in the church building. It was founded by Elisabeth Kübler-Ross, a world-renowned psychiatrist best known for changing how the medical profession dealt with people who were dying and the support their families received. My mother became good friends with her and quickly became one of the facilitators for the local group.

The group had a new-age, metaphysical undertone. I recall my mother asking me to go to the backyard and find a rock so that one of her friends could read the energy from the rock and predict my future. At ten years old, I was young enough that this did not confuse or alter my views of Christianity. I thought it was all the same—people being nice to each other. The adults in this group became like family to me as it was the first truly peaceful time I experienced in my life.

We still attended the Congregational church behind our house, and life smoothed out considerably. My mother stopped physically abusing me. She had a great support group of friends who offered help and guidance. I was in therapy as well, with the same new-age group. When I was in the third grade, I was registered into Cub Scouts, and that further expanded our family's social circle. My parents became friends with my Cub Scout leader, Lynn, and her husband, and our families spent a lot of time together. Lynn also ran a Bible study group that she invited my mother to.

Life was fine and dandy for a few years until I was in seventh grade and one of the women at the Bible study introduced my mother to a new religion. The flourishing faith called "born again" or Pentecostal was much like the Billy Graham Crusade or the 700 Club, which were huge televised evangelical church services. My mother slowly detached from the Congregational church and shifted her attendance to a different church.

She also tried to convert her new-age friends to become "born again" and accept Jesus Christ into their lives as their everlasting Savior. If they didn't choose to accept Jesus Christ into their hearts and lives, she believed they were going to be condemned to hell for eternity. When they were not receptive to her witnessing zeal, she abruptly ended all contact with the Friends of Shanti, including all of the therapy I was accustomed to receiving through them. Even though this group had supported her through overcoming her abusive behaviors, Mom completely rejected them since her new faith deemed their beliefs the work of Satan. She got frustrated and abruptly stormed out of the room.

I had spent time with adult friends for years, many of whom intervened in my mother's struggles to avoid abusing me, but now I was told it was inappropriate to visit them. Ever. After we got home, Mom rounded on me and for the first time in a long time, and I could see a flicker of the old, angry mom in her face (though this time she did it with a fake smile). In a low but stern voice, she said, "Those people are of the devil. Their beliefs are evil. And you are never to visit them again."

I didn't listen to her. For the first time in my life, I started to rebel. These were the same women who brought my mother refuge and provided me with a safe haven. I couldn't just let go of that stability, and for the first time, I didn't allow my mother to take it. I went behind her back, secretly meeting some of the women on a regular basis. There was a woman named Sandy whom I grew extremely fond of. Before her new change of heart, my mother would pawn me off on her when she needed alone time. Sandy was in school studying to be a child psychologist. She would take me to the movies, amusement parks, art fairs, and craft shows. She was truly one of the kindest, most caring individuals. Sadly, she was a victim of sexual abuse by a family member. This is what made her so compassionate about my own situation.

Many years later, when my mom found out that I was still staying in contact with Sandy, she exploded in rage. She demanded that Sandy come over to the house. When she arrived, my mother had members of the church seated in the living room, and I was asked to come down from my room to join. I could feel the tension building as six people started to gang up on Sandy, threatening her with a restraining order, accusing her of molesting me. Inside I was frozen. I could not believe what I was witnessing. My own mother was blatantly and falsely accusing an innocent woman of molesting her son. Sandy tried everything to maintain her composure until she couldn't take it any longer. That's when I jumped in: "Mom, this is beyond inaccurate. How low can you actually go knowing everything Sandy's been through, sharing with you her deepest family nightmare, and now you have the audacity to use it against her?"

No response, no reaction, nothing. My mother stood firm as if she truly believed her own lies. That's when I knew I had lost my own mother to what I felt was an occult society.

My father was not pleased about this new conversion, which he considered just a drain on the finances. He wasn't happy primarily because my mother was writing checks to the new church. He pulled my brother and me aside and said that it was a phase our mom was going through and it would pass.

Or not.

About a year later, I came home from hanging out with friends and walked into the house to see my father standing in a circle with a bunch of my mother's friends from her new church. They were speaking in tongues and screaming, "Praise Jesus! Hallelujah Jesus! Accept Jesus Christ into the heart of Raymond!" It crushed me to know that I had just lost my father the same way I had lost my mother the year before. Instead of their religious conversion enhancing our home and lives, my relationship with them became more confrontational and tense. They were more combatants than parents.

Let the escalation begin. This was not exactly what I had in mind for my teenage years. With my father now thoroughly entrenched in this newfound religion, parental religious brainwashing became the new normal for Darin and I. For my part, I wasn't buying it. So, I started spending more time away from home: going to the library, immersing myself in after-school activities—the one staple I still had left.

I continued to attend the same Congregational church as always, but now only with my grandmother. I was sad that the family photo for the church directory was eventually just me, a family of one. I felt a definite connection and camaraderie within that religious community that I wanted to continue, and I wanted to be a good Christian boy. I had an internal intuition that my parents' newfound religion was superficial and showy. I felt it disrespected God to be hollering, "Jesus, save me!" while jumping around and waving arms. I figured my parents were trying to be good people of faith, but this particular church affiliation didn't sit well with me.

Chapter 2

A Study in Contradictions

I firmly believe that we cannot tolerate discrimination
against any individuals or groups in our country.
Such treatment always brings with it pain
and perpetuates hate and intolerance.[2]

~ Barbara Bush

Content warning: This chapter depicts a violent hate crime.

Through the ups and downs of my parents' faith journey, there was an undercurrent in my life that I didn't know how to deal with. I knew it was expected that as an adult, I would have a beautiful home, a wife, and children. From a young age, I was aware of that societal expectation. When we were little, my friend Katie and I played "house" together. We flipped through catalog pages, choosing patio furniture and other home accessories. It would be like the TV sitcom *Leave It to Beaver*. Lots of people thought Katie and I would get married when we grew up.

But I had one huge problem. I always knew there was something different about me. As a child, I did not identify it with a particular word. However, my life revolved around a word that had not yet been introduced into my vocabulary.

Others weren't so blind, though. When I was in fourth grade, my class was lining up to go to lunch. One of my male classmates was standing in front of me. Several other students noticed me staring at his rear end and started to make fun of me. "Yuck, that's disgusting. Dennis was staring at another guy's butt," one said. I was so shocked and frightened that I made extremely sure that I never stared at another boy at school again.

In seventh grade, we had a substitute teacher. Some students were calling her a lesbian, gossiping and mimicking her. I asked another teacher what the word *lesbian* meant. She pulled me aside and asked why I wanted to know, so I shared with her what the other students were saying about the substitute. She said, "Dennis, the word *lesbian* is defined as a woman who has romantic feelings for another woman and engages in a same-sex physical relationship."

I replied, "That's just like the word *gay* stands for two men loving each other."

"Yes." I knew right then that from that moment on that I would be battling with my feelings toward other men.

Because I was still so young, sexual orientation had never been specifically explained to me, but children are neither deaf nor stupid. I had heard enough from the adults around me, as well as from other children and teens, to know that homosexuality was considered bad, abnormal, and deviant. I underwent a terrific struggle within myself. I could not conceive of identifying myself as gay because just the idea disgusted me—as I had been taught that it should. But the thought that I might be gay was becoming more and more prevalent in my mind. So much so that within a week, I was on a frantic rampage to find pornographic magazines to convince myself that I could be physically attracted to females. I rode my bicycle to neighborhood stores, asking if I could purchase *Playboy* or *Penthouse*. Since I was a minor, no one would sell me anything.

I did not give up. I had a friend at school whose father read dirty magazines. I gave my classmate a dollar, and he handed over a whole stack of them. All of the magazines had risqué photos of women in them, but some featured similar photos of men as well.

I walked home that evening, went up to my room, closed my door, and desperately tried to find pleasure in ogling the photos of the women. But the longer I stared, the more obvious it became: nothing was happening. I became angry and hurt that I could not desire something classified as "normal." I also felt deeply betrayed because the attraction I felt for the men in the magazines confirmed what I didn't want to believe.

Frustrated and confused, with incontrovertible evidence still before my eyes, I believed there was something wrong with me and questioned my basic self-worth. My mind was a hurricane of thoughts. *Why would God make me like this? If it's so wrong, why do I feel it? I didn't ask for this to happen! I've done everything I can!* Tears rolled down my face, and I hoped with my whole soul that this attraction was nothing more than a temporary phase. Because I wanted nothing more than for the feelings and thoughts to go away.

As you can tell from the title of this book, they did not go away. And during my preteen and teen years, I had fantasies of holding another man close. Falling asleep at night, holding my pillow, I thought about having a relationship with a man with whom I could feel safe, comfortable, and in love. I imagined waking up next to him and hoped there was someone out there waiting for me, as I would only settle for a monogamous relationship. I only allowed myself to think about this during private moments at night. I was still very much conflicted. Internally, I thought of how wonderful it would be to have a family with another man who accepted me exactly as I am and loved me for that. Externally, I knew that to be socially accepted, I needed to find a nice gal, settle down, and start a family. I know now that this is what causes so many men and women to enter into heterosexual marriage even while knowing they are gay—because they want to be accepted by their families and friends.

I continued to suppress my feelings, ashamed and scared that my fellow students would identify me as different or gay. And I tried to walk the walk, as it were. During my freshman year of high school, I met my first girlfriend at a mutual friend's birthday party. We talked between classes at school, held hands, and did the usual things that teenagers do—with one exception: I was never able to convince myself to give her a kiss. She broke off the relationship two weeks later.

That same year, it was time to start attending confirmation classes. Even though my parents had switched to the Pentecostal church, I still continued to attend the Congregational church. I got up every Sunday morning and put on my best clothes: an ironed polo shirt, dress slacks, and penny loafers with argyle socks. Confirmation classes were after school on Mondays with lessons from the scriptures about being a good person. You would think that my parents would be proud that their son was committed to following Christian beliefs, went to church every Sunday, and even devoted Mondays after school to learn the teachings of God through the Bible.

Nope! On the outside, all appeared normal. What happened inside the house was a different story. One Sunday in particular, my parents asked me to go to brunch. I agreed, but instead I was taken to a Sunday afternoon session at their Pentecostal establishment. I was placed in a room with the doors locked and confronted by many pastors, stating I did not have Jesus Christ in my heart and that I would not receive everlasting love and acceptance into heaven. I think there was some suspicion on my mother's part that I might be gay, even though I did not accept or understand the mere thought of it in myself, and I had certainly never mentioned it even being part of my life. I felt my parents had joined an organization that used brainwashing techniques to find your individual weaknesses and offer a solution that only they could provide.

Shortly after that, I woke up late for school on a Friday morning, flustered and worried. My parents said they were keeping me out of school to take a day trip to the shoreline. I was baffled that my father was home from work on a weekday but proceeded to get in the shower for what I thought was to be was a fun day with my parents. I was a very organized teenager—I ironed my clothes every Sunday night to last me through the week. I knew exactly what I was going to wear: a black polo shirt and khakis. When I was done showering, I opened my closet to find a lot of my clothes missing, including my planned shirt. I turned to my father. "What's going on?"

"Calm down, son. It's going to be okay."

I had a gut-wrenching feeling that something wasn't right. After we were already in the car, they said I was being committed to a psychiatric hospital for troubled teens to receive correction therapy. Correction for what? Was this really about faith and church attendance? Did they suspect that I'm gay? At the facility, I learned that a psychiatrist and psychologist I had never seen had signed paperwork certifying that I was a threat to myself and others. There were some discrepancies as dates, times, and years did not match certain records. Apparently, my parents had someone from their church with the appropriate credentials create the documents stating they had multiple visits with me when, in fact, we had never met.

I was mortified when it also came to my attention that my mother had a meeting with my confirmation class, telling them that I was going away to seek mental health conversion treatment, and with that help, I would come back a different person.

After trying to explain to the institution that I was wrongfully committed, I knew I had no hope other than prayer and guidance from our Heavenly Father. I frantically tried to find people I could trust to believe my story, but to no avail. I realized it was time to fake it till you make it. I had to pretend to come around to the conclusion that I would join the Pentecostal church, but asked that my parents please allow me to continue my confirmation with the Congregational church. After the confirmation in May, I would switch churches. I knew I couldn't have this "revelation" overnight, so I had to act slowly. Six weeks later, I was finally released. To this day, I still thank God that I did not go through any kind of electroshock therapy, as I saw the damage it caused my own mother.

Lights, camera, action. Returning home was an internal emotional roller coaster. I was now the director on set performing new parts every day that had no scripts, only improv. Every scene was filled with a rotating cast of characters and acts like the three-ring circus was in town. My poor brother was so quiet and reserved. He didn't know what to think.

In May 1988, I was confirmed into the Congregational church and allowed to receive my first communion. It was a magnificent day. My parents threw a huge party, and over sixty family members and friends attended. I felt like it was a Bar Mitzvah or pre-wedding party. Everyone was there to celebrate my statement of commitment to God.

I did not, as I had promised, begin to attend the Pentecostal church with my parents after my confirmation, and the pressure picked up again. I wasn't conforming to what they wanted. There were repeated instances of my parents basically blackmailing me to go to church with them. They would invite me to go on outings with them and then drive me to their church, just to be screamed at by religious fundamentalists about Jesus "saving" me from myself. I continued to hold off even when my parents threatened to have me committed to the psychiatric hospital again.

I'd had enough. The movie *Irreconcilable Differences* gave me the idea of divorcing my parents, so I learned what I needed to do to become emancipated and given rights in a court of law to be my own legal guardian. But I had to wait until my sixteenth birthday, which wasn't until that August.

A few days after starting summer break, my parents became aware of the fact that I wanted to become emancipated. I even recalled over-hearing my parents talking with members of their church about send-ing me to a camp in Missouri. My own mind was spinning out of control. *If I end up in Missouri, I could be stuck there until I'm eigh-teen.* A discussion elevated quickly to an argument that caused me to fear being locked up prior to turning sixteen, preventing me from separating myself from my parents. I felt that I had no choice. I ran into the garage to grab my bicycle and started riding to a friend's house. I was officially a runaway. I was fortunate to have the great network of friends that had previously been close to my mother before her Pentecostal conversion, and they took me in. One couple even considered sending me to California to stay with their extended family to wait out the last two months before my sixteenth birthday until I could be emancipated.

August 1988, my high school social worker, my best friend, and a few adults from my support network took me to juvenile court to plead my case in front of a judge. I was able to prove that I was respon-sible to take care of my own needs as a legal adult. I now had all the rights of an adult.

Oh my goodness, it was my sixteenth birthday and I now had the legal rights of a twenty-one-year-old.

As I entered my sophomore year in high school, I was my own legal guardian. I rented an apartment from one of the families in the Friends of Shanti group. Since we were so close to New York City, I was already working occasionally as a model for print advertising and TV commercials and had enough income to support myself. The school administration had no clue what to do with me.

I was an active member of many school clubs, including the French club, Russian club, Future Business Leaders of America, DECA (Distributive Education Club of America, a club that fosters business activity and marketing), and the drama club. I was the president of the Human Relations Council, a group of students who helped integrate the seventy-six different nationalities we had in our town. The only minority we were never taught about was the group of individuals classified as having same-sex orientation. It was not even discussed.

Through these clubs, I developed many friendships, especially with a girl named Julie. We became best friends, and I found great joy having her in my life. Because we were attached at the hip, people perceived us as an item. But one thing was missing between Julie and me. We never kissed, never held hands, never shared a physically intimate moment.

One day, Julie and I were watching our favorite show together, the *Oprah Winfrey Show*. The episode featured two male bodybuilders and well-known weight trainers, one of whom had previously won the Mr. Universe competition. It was their coming-out show. I couldn't believe that right there in front of my very own eyes were two drop-dead gorgeous, masculine bodybuilders openly saying on national TV that they were gay! The only portrayals I'd seen of gay men on screen—TV or movies—were over-the-top crossdressers, extremely effeminate men, or unattractively fat and bald men. This was a total surprise. For the first time, I realized that openly gay people look and act as normal as everyone else. The exaggeration of walking with a hip-swaying sashay was just for TV.

But I had to put up a front for Julie. She started giggling and said, "Yuck, that's disgusting."

I replied nervously, agreeing, "All of this is horrible. How could anyone do that?" I was so fearful that she would see my interest in these two beautiful men, but I could not take my eyes off the screen. I knew at that time I couldn't confess my true feelings about my sexuality to Julie. For her part, she may have suspected already anyway since we never had any physical contact but had no idea how to ask.

I tried to maintain a relationship with my parents even after moving out of our family's home and occasionally went there to spend time with them. Sooner rather than later, it was all in the open. October 11 has been designated National Coming Out Day, and I was at my parents' house watching TV with my mom after school. I certainly had not planned to say anything to her, but that day, the *Oprah Winfrey Show* had a presentation about LGBT people and coming out. My mom wrinkled her nose.

"They are all going to hell. That is so disgusting."

I looked over at her and stopped myself from rolling my eyes. "Really? You think that's disgusting?"

"Yes, I do. They're going to hell. It's in the Bible." She stopped and stared hard at me. "You're gay, aren't you." It was a statement, not a question.

I hesitated, but I had nothing else to say. "Yes."

"I knew it!" she burst out. "I always knew it! Your father is going to be livid when he gets home!"

I wasn't there when he got home.

My mother wasn't the only person to figure it out. Two weeks later, on October 25, 1989, I walked into the men's room at school. Fifteen boys were present although a rule said there should only be a maximum of eight students at a time in a restroom. A hall monitor was outside reading a book.

I was using the urinal when I heard several derogatory comments behind me. "That f******* f***** should not be allowed to live!" Suddenly someone kicked me in the back, smashing my face into the wall. Other boys shouted, "People like that should not be allowed in this school!" "That f***** is lucky I don't hurt him!"

Suddenly, all of them started screaming the slur at me, almost like a chant. I tried to get away, but they blocked the door and shut off the lights. I was cornered in the dark bathroom with five attackers taking turns punching my face, jaw, and stomach. Blood was pouring down my neck, onto my clothing, and the floor. Another ten or so boys were yelling and cheering them on.

As soon as the hall monitor opened the door, I was picked up by my shirt and thrown out of the lavatory by one of my assailants. The monitor, scheduled to retire at the end of the week, tried to stop the attackers but he was too fragile to even hope of stopping them.

The attackers poured out the doorway screaming, "I'm gonna f******* kill you!"

Fearing for my life, I scrambled for the Mace on my key chain and blindly sprayed as much as I could in the direction of my attackers. With the barrage halted, I ripped myself away and bolted for the administrative offices. One of the secretaries handed me a towel to stop the bleeding and another called security while I hysterically stammered out what had just happened.

When the guards and administration arrived, I was still hyperventilating from pain and severe shock. I tried to catch my breath and explain, but the vice principal interrupted me. "I don't care. You should not have gone around Mace-happy."

Stunned, I sat down outside her office. I overheard her talking to the hall monitor, saying that this incident would never have occurred if I dressed differently and made out with girls in the hallway. I was forced to wait an hour in the administrative suite before I was escorted into the nurse's office. The reason, I found out later, was that the boys who had so cruelly beaten me were being taken care of first.

The vice principal finally came to speak to me. "You're lucky we don't have you arrested. We are going to suspend you for a few days." Then I was dismissed to go to the hospital to be treated for the multiple injuries I received during the attack.

This second attack by the vice principal was on my mental and emotional capacities rather than my body, but it was just as real and just as debilitating. I had survived being viciously beaten by a mob, and now I was abandoned by the school administration that should have supported me. I had to drive myself to the emergency room, and the rest of my high school education was in jeopardy.

While I was suspended, I was contacted by the local newspaper and a television news program. I never learned how they knew about the attack, but they found me and interviewed me about the attack and the administration's response. I did not seek them out. After the school system found out about my interviews, an administrator called me and said politely, "Why don't we get together? There's no need for you to go to the newspapers. We can work this whole thing out."

I never mentioned to any reporter the words "gay bashing," or that I was attacked for being gay. I was still in denial about my own sexuality. I did confirm that I had sprayed Mace in self-defense after being brutally attacked.

The following morning, I was allowed to return to school. However, because of the hate-filled threats I continued to receive, I was assigned a security guard to escort me to classes. Rumors were flying throughout my school of 1,800 students. I was not allowed to use the student lavatories; I had to use the faculty restrooms.

After school officials saw me in the media a second time, I was told that I would be put on homebound tutoring, receiving ten hours a week of instruction to fulfill my curriculum requirements. How could ten hours be enough to compensate for a week's worth of schooling? What would I do without interaction with my friends? What would happen with my participation in all of those after-school clubs I belonged to? Who was going to be the president of the Human Relations Council? I agreed because I was led to believe that it would last only a month or so. However, all of my extracurricular participation was simply taken away from me, and I remained on homebound tutoring for the rest of the school year.

It got worse after I appeared on national television. At the end of December, I received a phone call from a producer of *The Sally Jessy Raphael Show*, then a prominent national talk show, asking me to appear and tell my story. I said no. I would rather drop dead than tell the whole world that I was the victim of a gay bashing.

I called my school social worker, who had also helped with my emancipation proceedings, to tell her about the request and that I had declined their invitation. She said, "Do you realize that in the past year, 57 percent of all crimes committed in public high schools and 33 percent of all suicides committed by teenagers were based on sexual-identity issues?"

The mental light bulb flashed on. Could I accept my own sexual orientation for the purpose of helping others? What if I could help even just one person? That would matter. Besides, I reasoned, how many people were actually going to see the show anyway? Most people I knew had full-time jobs and all my classmates would be in school. I had no idea how many people actually watched *Sally Jessy Raphael*, nor did I think about that new invention called the VCR. I was naïve enough to genuinely believe that nobody I knew in real life would ever find out.

It went viral without the internet.

The show aired January 19, 1990. I'll never forget the guest who appeared at my side as I told my story. She was Mary Griffith, the mother of Bobby Griffith, who was an all-American boy . . . and he was gay. He was faced with an irresolvable conflict in that his mother and her faith taught him that to be gay was wrong and he couldn't accept who he was. So at age twenty in 1983, he chose to take his own life. His mother, who had been very militant in her faith and had prayed that her son would be "healed" from homosexuality, was traumatized by his suicide. By the time we appeared on TV together, she had transformed herself into a national crusader in behalf of gay and lesbian youth.

Oh my goodness, the team producing this show really knew how to get the ratings. Placing Mary directly beside me after the commercial break was definitely not coincidental as I talked about my fundamentally religious parents not accepting or approving of what they called a "chosen lifestyle."

Sometime between the taping of the show and when it aired, I received two phone messages from an officer with the local police department. The first message said that it was urgent that I contact

Dennis on The Sally Jessy Raphael Show *in 1990*

her. The second message said, "Dennis, there is a warrant out for your arrest. Either you turn yourself in or I will be forced to come and get you."

I was charged with five counts of assault and two counts of risk of injury to a minor. Allegedly, five people were infected by the fumes from the Mace I used in self-defense. I was five feet, eight inches tall and weighed 135 pounds. How could someone so small do so much damage to students who were twice my size, some of whom were on the football team?

I was released on a $2,000 non-security bond. Because I was legally an emancipated minor, my parents were not obligated to help me, and they did not offer. I had to find an attorney myself. The case was brought to court, and I pleaded not guilty to the assault charge, which was a felony. After eighteen months of continuations and numerous court appearances, the charges were dropped. I attribute this, in part, to my extensive media connections.

My initial appearance on *The Sally Jessy Raphael Show* was so sensational that *Larry King Live* from CNN took an interest in me as well and booked me for January 30, 1990. Sally Jessy Raphael then asked me to reappear on her show on April 5, 1990, to tell my story again.

That led to appearances on seven talk shows and reports in many newspaper articles, both locally and nationally. Although the media embellished a lot, much of what was said was the truth. I seized the opportunity to show others in similar situations how to stand up for themselves and what they believed in. This entire experience of the attack, the administration response, and the media reports and appearances had a major impact in shaping who I have become.

Much of this ordeal could have been avoided had there been a law in place in my state against hate crimes. In 1990, *Dennis on* Larry King Live *in 1990*

such a bill was being considered by the state legislature. A lobbyist who was working to get the bill passed contacted me and asked if I would testify before the Judiciary Committee. I immediately agreed to do anything I could to ensure passage of the bill.

The day finally arrived, and I walked into the legislative office building feeling nervous and empowered at the same time. The hearing room was packed. I waited hours for my turn to speak, a span that seemed like days. Once I sat in front of the committee, I tried to read the notes in front of me but was unable to. The frightening emotions of that horrific day returned in force and made my entire body shake. Amazingly, I did not cry but instead summoned the strength to compose myself. I was determined to tell them everything—that I had been attacked by a gang of fifteen students in my high school because of my sexual orientation, that they had not been arrested or disciplined in any way, and that I had been arrested for using Mace in self-defense. It was all a blur. I was so emotional after testifying that I didn't stay to hear the results of the committee vote. I watched it on the TV news that evening. The bill was written to include all minorities in addition to LGBT individuals. For example, it would be prosecuted as a hate crime with stronger penalties if someone painted a swastika on a Jewish synagogue, rather than treated as minor graffiti.

The Connecticut hate crimes bill took effect in October 1991. I am proud to have participated in the process that led to the enactment of this important piece of legislation. Had the law been in effect at the time of my attack, those boys could have been charged with a felony.

As I compose this narrative almost thirty years later, tears run down my face because I still have vivid flashbacks of the attack. I remember exactly what happened as if it were an hour ago. It makes me wonder about how barbaric people can be. When will this intolerance change? How does hate develop into such horrific violence against people minding their own business? Why do we have to pass laws to tell people not to hate? I don't expect everyone to accept who I am, but why do those who cannot accept LGBTs have to beat and bloody them to placate their hate for anyone different from themselves?

I have been able to forgive those who attacked me in high school and called me names in the hallways while changing classes, the school administrative personnel who could not support me when I was struggling with my identity and in my time of extreme need, and those who just did not understand what it was like to be different. I found out who my true friends were, and I appreciate all those who stood behind me.

We all have key events in our lives that bring us to new levels of understanding. These help mold the kind of people we become later in life. The attack and my time in the bright lights changed me forever, but that did not mean my new way of accepting my sexuality was strewn with flowers.

In so many ways, I decided to be a survivor, not a victim, and to use the journey of my life as a source of inspiration to help others in similar situations.

Chapter 3

O Beloved Brother

To love another person is to see the face of God.[3]

~ Jean Valjean

My brother, Darin, was the first person who gained a true understanding of who I really am as a person, who saw me as a beloved child of our Heavenly Father. He was four years younger than me, so I was very protective of him. But those roles reversed as he got older, even though I was older and the one who was supposed to provide him with wisdom and comfort. I always felt safe around him because I knew I could share anything with him and not be judged. He was one of those brothers who would keep even the deepest of secrets. He always understood and lent an ear to just listen. Later in life, he would bring much wisdom to some of my most complex experiences.

He was always a Goody Two-shoes, a quiet kid. But his laugh was infectious and made everyone around him laugh as well. One of my fondest memories is from when we went to Disney World as a family. At EPCOT, he was mesmerized by the smallest things, like the water jumping at the science center. He would try to catch it. Even today, I laugh just thinking about it.

We had lovely times together when we were kids. Our family vacationed at a cottage in the mountains, and I taught Darin to swim in the lake. Our parents would go out bowling on Friday nights and leave the two of us home together. I allowed him to do things that he wouldn't otherwise get away with, like stay up past his bedtime and watch "bad" TV shows. As soon as we heard the garage door opening, he would run to bed and pretend to be asleep.

He first stepped up as my support in January 1990, a few days after I had gone to New York City to film my first appearance on *The Sally Jessy Raphael Show*. He was home sick from school one day, and I knew I should tell him the situation even though he was barely thirteen and in middle school. I didn't want him to hear from his peers that his brother had come out to the world as gay on national television. He was lying on the couch and watching TV when I approached him. I was a nervous wreck, thinking he wouldn't understand or be supportive because of his age. At his age, I didn't even know what the word *gay* was. But he needed to know what was happening to me because it would affect him as well.

"Darin, I have to talk to you about something serious. I need to share why I went to New York."

He looked up. "You were doing some modeling for TV commercials, right?"

"Not exactly. Do you remember last October when I was beaten up in school?"

"Of course I do. I wish I was there and it never would have happened."

I took a deep breath. "Well, you don't know the truth about why I was attacked. I was accused of being gay, and that's why I was assaulted. I downplayed the attack so you wouldn't know what had really happened."

Darin sat up, very angry. "Are you kidding me? No one should get away with this to my own brother. Oh, I could kill them!" And then this otherwise-reserved child let loose a string of swear words on my behalf.

"Well, Darin, it's true though. I am gay." He was the easiest person to come out to.

"So what? They need to pay for what they did to my brother." His freckled face was a furious shade of red. His complete acceptance of my situation hit me like a freight train. I couldn't have sat and examined that more in the moment if I wanted to, so I just kept going.

I told him that I had gone on a TV show to tell the world what had happened, airing the dirty laundry about what had occurred at my high school along with sharing our family's circumstances. "I told them why I became emancipated and our parents being fundamentalist religious fanatics. No holds barred."

"Why? Why would you say all that on TV?"

"If it could help even just one person to avoid what I went through, then in my mind, it was worth it."

He relaxed back into his pillow. "Cool. I support that, and most important, I support you. I don't care if you're gay. In fact, it makes me love you more." He seemed to have more knowledge and compassion of the subject than I had expected.

I felt like I should warn him about receiving backlash himself. "You're going to have some ridicule from your classmates. You understand how kids can be."

"Yes, I do." He nodded. "I'm a big boy, and I can handle myself."

I just hugged him. What had I done to deserve a brother like this? Years later, I found out from a cousin that he had indeed dealt with a lot of ridicule and cruelty at school over my situation and actions, but he never let on. It could not have been easy for someone so young, especially in that era. Hearing some of the things he confronted even led me to feel somewhat responsible for what was to come later down the path.

When I graduated from high school, Darin was just entering as a freshman. He decided to go to a technical school instead of the regular high school. I was never told why he made that choice, but it's certainly plausible that he was not interested in going to the same school I had just left, wanting to avoid following my reputation and recent catapult into the national spotlight.

When he graduated four years later, I was living about two hours away near Boston. I attended the school ceremonies with our parents and grandparents, and they put together a huge party. It was an especially big deal because I had chosen to not participate in my own high school graduation for fear of being mocked and possibly attacked again.

It was wonderful to see Darin with all of his buddies. He had a job lined up to work for a locksmith firm, where he'd already done a yearlong apprenticeship. My mother had Darin's business cards displayed and a marvelous description of his accomplishments, all accompanied by a Bible scripture.

Graduation Celebration for
Darin Scott Schleicher
Cheney Regional Technical School
June 13, 1995
Major: Carpentry
Employment: Locksmith for
Manchester/Vernon Safe & Lock

"Do not store up for yourselves treasures on earth, where moths and vermin destroy, and where thieves break in and steal. But store up for yourselves treasures in heaven, where moths and vermin do not destroy, and where thieves do not break in and steal. For where your treasure is, there your heart will be also."
~ NIV Matthew 6:19–21

Heavenly Father, how wonderful is the capacity to grow and to learn, to discover truth in the world, and add good knowledge to our lives. Today we especially thank you for this important milestone in Darin's life. We thank you for the rewards of his hard work and persistent studies. We thank you for all the possibilities that lie ahead and that by your Grace we have a future and a hope. In the years to come, Lord, remind Darin of all the gifts he has so freely received from you. Give him the courage and strength to persevere through tasks and to achieve goals. But most of all, we pray for the molding and perfection of character that comes only from the work of the Holy Spirit as we allow him free rein in our hearts. Take this life, Lord, and guide it, even protecting Darin in your loving arms.

I was equally as proud of Darin as my parents were, especially about the accolades he received from the owners of the locksmith firm. But this kind of praise was definitely something I never would have received from them, even if I had chosen to participate in my own high school graduation. I've never resented Darin for it, but I certainly felt undercut by our parents.

Even though Darin was considered a good Christian at my parents' church, he confided in me that it was just a show. He didn't feel he had a choice, so he put up a good front and pretended to go along with their beliefs. He'd already seen the lengths our parents had gone to in attempts to convince me to "convert" to their faith and wanted to avoid the same fate. He felt no emotional or spiritual connection with the members of that church or its teachings, so once his graduation was over and he was an adult, he never stepped foot in that building again.

Personally, I was at a point that I couldn't even look at a Bible—the hair on the back of my neck would prickle as I internally recoiled from what I perceived as the source of pain and turmoil in my life.

We were now both adults, and Darin and I remained as close as ever. He was the first person I called to help me in any situation. A few months after his graduation, I was breaking up with my partner and wanted to move out of our apartment immediately. Darin made a six-hour drive through a snowstorm with a U-Haul to move me from Massachusetts back to Connecticut—it would have taken only two hours in normal weather. He smoothed the way with our parents to allow me to move back into our childhood home temporarily, for the first time since I'd been emancipated. When I got to my new apartment, and at every new home I moved into after that, Darin always made sure to change the locks himself with top-end security features to ensure my safety.

As I climbed the ranks in my career, he was always happy for me with each new job I acquired. Our parents generally ignored my advancement and expressed no praise at all for my accomplishments, so it was especially heartwarming to receive support and encouragement from my brother.

I had a position as the director of education for a large professional hair care line and later switched to a different company as a district manager covering New England. Not long after that, I had just received a third callback interview for a traveling position selling hair products to salons and spas throughout Connecticut. I ran into my brother at the mall, where I could tell that he'd been working on changing locks for stores since he had his work gear with him. He gave me a huge hug as I told him about my new opportunity.

His face glowed with his enormous smile. "I'm so happy for you! Nobody deserves this more than you." We sat on a bench and talked for a few minutes. It was wonderful to catch up together. He was truly my best friend, someone who got me and always had my back.

The drama in my dating life did not seem to faze him one bit. And let me tell you, there was a *lot* of drama. One January, I had met someone at the grand opening of a department store. After two days of ribbon-cutting and other festivities, I stopped at a liquor store on my way home to purchase a bottle of wine. I did not drink alcohol on a regular basis, so after just a couple of glasses, it went to my head. I called Darin, and he immediately recognized a change in my voice. I guess that's what is referred to as drunk dialing. At least I called my brother and not The Guy.

Darin came over right away and found me stumbling around my kitchen and slurring my words. I was holding a rose and pulling off the petals. "Does he love me? He loves me not. Is he gay? My luck, is he straight?"

Darin just sat there watching me, trying to not laugh. "I don't think I've ever seen you drunk before. You're really funny! Well, you're also really funny without alcohol."

"Yeah, I am drunk! I found a Greek god, and I think I'm in love with him. I don't even know if he's gay or into me."

He listened to me ramble on for a while, occasionally interjecting things like, "Of course he's into you. You're a great catch!" The last thing I remember of that night is when he decided it was time for me to go to bed. He heaved me over his shoulder, carried me to my room, and dropped me onto the mattress. He made sure I was tucked in and said he'd call in the morning to check on me. The next morning, he showed up with coffee and aspirin. That's the kind of thoughtfulness you could always expect from my brother and his heart of gold.

As the turn of the century approached, Darin, our cousin Sarah, and a few friends decided to have a small gathering at my home on New Year's Eve. A good friend, Robin, provided much-needed entertainment that made Darin laugh as I'd never seen before. She was one of a kind and could always make people laugh. Her vivacious and outgoing personality was contagious. Unfortunately, she was developing liver damage due to alcohol use and just couldn't heed her doctor's warnings. She eventually passed away in 2005 from liver failure. At the time, we knew she was an alcoholic, and Darin and I vowed to each other to never end up like that.

That promise is what makes the next part so dreadful.

This event is imprinted in my head like it was carved in Vermont granite. It was 8:30 on a Tuesday morning in mid-March. I was driving with the vice president of one of the hair care lines I represented to visit some of my top accounts that day. I was on the phone with my mother, and I could tell by her voice that things were not in sync.

"Mom, you need to tell me what's going on," I insisted.

"Something's been off with Darin. Your father and I couldn't quite put our finger on it until we received a phone call from the parents of Darin's best friend. They told us that they no longer want him hanging around with their son. He's been struggling with cocaine addiction and has been in and out of rehab. Every time Darin comes around, he has a relapse."

"You're kidding. What did Darin have to say about this?"

"He told us to mind our own business, and he has it under control."

"Mom, Darin is twenty-four years old. It's unusual to develop that kind of drug addiction at this age. People are usually introduced to it in high school or college. What are you going to do?"

"We've consulted with our church's pastor. He said all we can do is pray, and everything will be fine." That was my parents' answer to everything—just pray and it will all work out. I rejected that approach and knew Darin would too. If he was in fact addicted to drugs, he needed professional help.

I started to see a change in Darin as he used drugs on a more frequent and regular basis. I learned that Darin had been introduced to marijuana earlier in life by a friend. That was the gateway drug that eventually led to crack and cocaine. I ultimately had to involve my aunts and uncles to get Darin into rehabilitation and treatment centers. It all took a toll on my parents—it seemed like I was watching them age ten years right before my eyes. I learned later that my mother and father almost left their church because they were getting such poor advice about how to manage Darin's addictions and rehabilitation treatment, but they stuck it out.

Three and a half years passed with the same story over and over. Darin would enter rehab, declaring that he would never do any drugs again, only to relapse within weeks or months. He described to me once that when he was high, it was as if he was stuck behind a six-foot glass wall. He could see the world and would try to touch it, but he couldn't reach it.

As difficult as Darin's situation was, life for me continued on. In late 2003, I started a new position that was responsible for millions of dollars in sales. My job was demanding, but I loved it—flying all over to conduct meetings, working with distributors and management, wining and dining my sales reps, and attending hair shows in every major city in the country. But behind my business persona, I was embarrassed to have a brother who was a drug addict. My embarrassment stemmed from my own insecurity of being guilty by association. I was afraid my sales reps, managers, and marketing department would assume I was also on drugs if I were being funny or just my normal ditzy self. I can be a stereotypical spacey blond at times—I do have my moments.

On Mother's Day in 2004, my aunt hosted a celebration and barbecue at her house. Darin was out of rehab and drove his quad around the property, giving rides to my younger cousins. My mother was elated that he was clean and sober again.

The next week, my parents left for Vermont on vacation, which was the same day I had an afternoon flight to Ohio for a ten-day business trip. As I was preparing to leave, I had a nagging feeling to stop by their house to check on Darin, since they were already gone. It started in the morning and continued throughout the day. I left my home for the airport and went past their exit off the freeway, still with a burning desire to turn around and go see Darin. I ignored my intuition. I wanted to get to the airport early so I wouldn't have to worry about rushing, and I could take some time to work on my laptop while waiting to board the flight.

When my flight landed, my colleague Kelly picked me up at curbside. As I was loading my luggage into the car, a heavy bag slid and fell on my toe. I let out a screech of pain and waved my arms in exasperation, and then my watch caught my eye—it was 7:11 p.m. The numbers seven and eleven together were significant to Darin and me. When we were little, people would comment on us being adorable and ask our ages. Our mother would say, "Seven and eleven, just like the convenience store." I came across those numbers randomly and often. If I saw that number combination somewhere, I knew that Darin was thinking about me or I was thinking about him.

From that moment, I was tremendously unsettled, knowing that I had done wrong by not listening to my intuition earlier and stopping to check on my brother. I learned later that my father was in a similar situation at the same time. My parents were at a lodge in Vermont to order dinner with their friends. The waitress had asked, "What would you like, sir?" three times, but he was in a daze. My mom asked multiple times if he was okay. He finally jerked out of it, but by that time both of my parents had a foreboding feeling that something wasn't right.

Sunday, May 16, 2004. I was in a business meeting when my phone kept ringing, and the caller ID showed it was my cousin Sarah. I ignored five or so calls, one right after another, until finally Kelly encouraged me to answer it since it was family.

I stepped out of the conference room and answered my phone. "Sarah, what's going on? You never call."

All I heard was repeated gasping of, "He's dead, he's dead, he's dead."

"Slow down, Sarah. What are you talking about?"

"My dad can't get ahold of your parents. Your dad isn't answering his cell phone."

"Sarah, slow down. What is happening?"

"I'm looking at your brother. I'm standing in the kitchen, looking down the stairs and seeing him hanging half out of the laundry room into the foyer." She was babbling and making no sense to me.

"Sarah, I don't understand."

"Darin's dead."

A sensation I cannot describe washed over my body, every muscle and nerve ending becoming paralyzed as I listened to my cousin ramble with information I was unable to comprehend. When she finished talking, I couldn't even hang up the phone because I was shaking so badly. Scrolling through my phone to find my dad's cell number seemed to take hours. When I finally connected, my dad answered immediately. I could hear my mother screeching in the background with a sound I'd never heard before or since—it was an indescribable sound of heartbreak and ultimate suffering, a piece of her soul being ripped apart. Hearing my own mother make a sound like that was forever seared into my mind.

My dad had just gotten off the phone with Uncle Jim, and they were immediately packing to leave Vermont and make the five-hour drive home. I told him I was in Columbus and would do whatever it took to get home as soon as possible, even if I had to rent a car and drive. It was Sunday evening, and finding an immediate flight would be challenging.

I pulled Kelly out of the meeting and told her what had just occurred. I was in complete shock. She grabbed me in a hug and held me tight, and I heard her mumble, "You need to be strong for them now." She sent me to my room to pack while she contacted the airlines, ordered a car, and checked me out of the hotel. She just took over and handled it all.

I was barely aware that I was leaving my entire team without any explanation, but Kelly would take care of that too. The news had not yet sunk in as I was shuffled off into the car and looked for my phone to call a close friend. The driver must have thought I was a nutcase as I sobbed through talking to her. I had to say it several times because I was almost unintelligible, and I didn't know the full details yet. All I knew was that my brother, my best friend, my emotional support for most of my life, was gone.

I arrived at the airport wearing dark sunglasses and tears streaming down my face. The ticket agent asked if everything was okay. I couldn't really answer, and she called security. The thought didn't even cross my mind that I might look suspicious—this was less than three years after 9/11. When security arrived, I had finally composed myself enough to speak clearly.

"I've just been told that my younger brother passed away, and I'm trying to get home."

The security personnel expressed condolences and left me alone, and the women behind the counter went to work. What a gift that they were able to work their magic. There was nothing direct, so they routed me all over the East Coast to get me home after five layovers. They even offered to put me in a quiet room so I could make phone calls and not be disturbed by the loudspeakers all over the airport.

During my first layover, I was told that my uncle had contacted my friend Alan, who owned two funeral homes in western Massachusetts. Actually, he was an ex-boyfriend I had dated for a year and a half. As if I needed something else to deal with. But my family didn't know about our relationship, so now I had to talk to a guy I hadn't spoken to in months. But I did. Alan was devastated at the news of Darin's passing and agreed to meet with my parents and me to make arrangements for Darin. My ex was now the funeral director for my brother's memorial service, and I didn't know how much more I could take. But Alan was extremely dignified and assured me that he would make sure my brother was well cared for.

I finally got home at 1:30 in the morning after completing a grand tour of US airports. I raced to my parents' house and hugged them both, but didn't stay long as I knew the next few days were going to be emotionally draining. I needed to go home and sleep for a while. I was still in so much shock and grief that I didn't sleep at all. I just lay there staring at the ceiling. After long sleepless hours, I eventually decided to get up at 5 a.m. and get on with the day.

I learned that once my grandmother had found Darin she immediately called 911 and was told to perform CPR on him until an ambulance arrived, but it was later determined that he had already been deceased for at least twenty hours. My grandmother called family to come to the house, and they waited together for the coroner to arrive and remove my brother's body from the property. My biggest concern had been that my mom and dad had seen the body of their son lying on the floor. Fortunately, the coroner was able to remove him before they arrived.

My aunts had cleaned up the vomit and most of the mess in the laundry room. They couldn't repair the plaster that had been torn off the wall from Darin grabbing the fixtures and falling. We believe that he knew he had overdosed and was trying to reach the phone to call for help. His legs were still inside the laundry room, and the rest of his body was stretched into the foyer where there was a phone just eight short feet from where he was lying. He had recently purchased a $150 fishing pole and was so excited to start the fishing season—this helps us know that it wasn't a suicide.

As the news spread of my brother's passing, the chaos was immense. I was juggling three phones—mine, my father's cell phone, and the house phone. Family, neighbors, and members of my parents' church poured in with food and condolences to offer comfort.

When my mother's sister arrived, we both just broke down in tears. She had also lost a son, but it had been in a random shooting when Darin and I were children. I remembered my mother gathering Darin and me to go to her house when we got the news.

Alan and his assistant from the funeral home came to the house to go over arrangements with my parents and me. He had one of his employees pick up Darin's body from the coroner's office to take it to his facility in Massachusetts for embalming and preparation for the funeral. He also rented a local funeral home in Glastonbury.

When Alan was ready to leave, my father pulled out his checkbook. "What do I owe you?"

"Mr. Schleicher, this is me, Dennis's friend. You can just pay for the cost of renting the funeral home." This was something I never saw coming. This was a guy I broke things off with—it was not a mutual separation and there had been a lot of drama. Now he was picking up the costs for my brother's funeral. Whatever had happened between us, Alan was and still is a devout Catholic with a heart full of compassion. He went above and beyond the usual expectations in preparing Darin's body for the viewing and funeral, and later allowed me extra access to the funeral home as part of my own grieving process.

Another blessing was the arrival of my Cub Scout leader, Lynn, and her husband, Dorino. Our families have been extremely close since we met when I was in third grade. In 1996, they lost their daughter in a car accident just a few blocks away from their blueberry farm. Carla's passing devastated both of her parents. My mother could now more fully relate to her best friend in the unbearable grieving of a parent burying their child.

Dorino had been born and raised in Italy and was a fourth-generation artisan who was an excellent craftsman in placing floor tiling. When he went to purchase a cemetery plot for his daughter, he was wearing his work clothes. The cemetery director haughtily told him that she could not be buried until everything was paid in full. Well, never judge a book by its cover. Dorino was extremely offended by the insinuation that he could not afford something for his child. He whipped out a handful of hundred dollar bills and, with his strong Italian accent, requested to reserve an entire section of the cemetery with over twenty burial plots.

Now he came to my parents. He talked about how Darin and Carla had grown up together and were close friends, so it would be his privilege to provide the cemetery plot so Darin could be buried out in the country next to Carla.

The next day, I went to Alan's funeral home up in Massachusetts because I wanted to style Darin's hair. No one knew how to do it like I did. It would be my first time seeing Darin's body since his passing, and I suppose it's thanks to Alan that I could face it at all.

When I first met Alan, I had an enormous fear of death. I figured the best way to overcome that fear was to go with him when his pager went off in the middle of the night to pick up a body at the hospital or nursing home or someone's house. He had employees to do this with him, but it was easier to not wake them up and do it myself. This was actually therapeutic to help me overcome my fear of dying and death. Of course, at the time, I had no comprehension that it was also preparing me to deal with the passing of my brother. Years later, I heard the saying that coincidences are when God chooses to remain anonymous.

When I arrived at the funeral home, I expected to see Darin in the embalming room, where the bodies are prepared for viewing. The side door to the funeral home was locked, which was odd because it's never locked. This is where distributors drop off caskets and florists leave the flower arrangements. When I called Alan's cell to let him know I was at the side door, he told me to go to the front entrance.

Entering the front door, the first thing I noticed was Darin's name prominently displayed. A guest book and cards were surrounded by flowers. Alan had again gone above and beyond the call of duty. Darin's body was already in the casket and set in the room for viewings. We had decided to have him dressed in his work uniform, because he had loved his job and felt so skilled and supported there. That was already done. As I fixed Darin's hair, I grieved over the loss of my brother before anyone else, including my parents, saw him. Oh, and did I need this time. Gazing at him with all that makeup made it so crushingly real that my younger brother and anchor had left this earth.

We woke the next morning to find Darin's obituary in the local newspaper and the official announcement produced another stabbing awareness of the reality of his passing.

I managed many more phone calls throughout the day, including one from Alan asking if I had contacted the police department about traffic control at the funeral home. I didn't think we needed to worry about it—I honestly didn't think Darin had many friends. I prepared myself for what I thought would be a short evening, but I was soon surprised.

The family had been told to come to the funeral home at 6 p.m. for a private viewing before the guests arrived. I realized it was a good thing I'd had private time with Darin the day before. I had no comprehension until then of the strength I needed to provide for my parents and grandmother. I saw cars pulling into the parking lot, but it barely registered. I took my mother by the arm, with my father on my other side and my grandmother next to him, and we almost staggered into the building under the weight of our grief.

We were greeted by an overflowing abundance of flowers. I had never seen this many flowers at any funeral I had ever been to, either someone I knew personally or at the funerals I attended with Alan. They were from so many friends and employers, even companies I hadn't worked for in quite some time.

The next thing I saw was my mother and relatives sobbing as their eyes were drawn to Darin's body displayed in the casket at the front of the room. For some people, the initial pain of a death will pass. But from what I've seen from our friends Lynn and Dorino, and now my parents, the pain and grief of separation due to a child's death is always there. My brother's been gone for fifteen years, and my parents have never been the same.

Dealing with the loss of a loved one is the hardest challenge that many of us face, as we are overcome by shock, confusion, and grief. I was experiencing this myself, and witnessing it firsthand in my family. My grandmother was the foundation that held everyone together that day. She stood there like a pillar, holding up the family as we watched a line form out the door and across the parking lot to the street.

Over the next four hours, we met almost a thousand people who came to pay their respects. I visited with relatives I hadn't seen in years. It's unfortunate that it takes a sad occasion such as a funeral to gather families together. I also saw friends from high school who traveled from out of state to support me in this time of sorrow. A good friend, Eileen, had even left her newborn baby with her husband in Philadelphia to come to the funeral.

Friends we never knew Darin had flooded the funeral home to share personal stories of Darin affecting and changing their lives with acts of kindness—offering people rides, buying them groceries, repairing their car, and even replacing their locks for free when they couldn't afford it. My parents and I had no idea. We could feel the outpouring of love as others shared testimonies of faith and respect for my brother. So many people placed red roses on his casket and offered hugs and condolences, and we all learned a different side of Darin that we never knew.

The funeral service the next day was held at my parents' church, which neither Darin nor I was comfortable with. This was the church that had tried to force me to convert to their version of Christianity when I was a teenager, and Darin had just kept his head down and gone along until he was an adult and could walk away. I knew in my heart of hearts that Darin would not like his funeral there, but our parents were in charge, and this was their church. I had tumultuous and mixed emotions about being there at all, compounded of course by the crushing sorrow of losing Darin.

My parents did show they cared for my grief in their own way. Two ministers gave sermons as part of the service, one from their church and the second from the Congregational church where I had received my confirmation. Even though I no longer attended there, that was the "home" church that I had grown up in.

The casket was removed from the hearse and brought into the church by the owners and staff of the locksmith firm, who we had asked to serve as pallbearers. The owners of the company had been forced to let Darin go several times during his addiction, but they always left the door open for him to return to work when he was sober. That spoke volumes to us.

A letter my father had written to my brother appeared in the church program:

Darin,

All night God has reminded me of this thought and this morning I searched and found a verse of scripture for you. "For I know the thoughts that I think towards you, says the Lord, thoughts of peace and not of evil, to give you a future and hope" (Jeremiah 29:11). Go to work in confidence knowing God's desire for you is good. You will remain in my thoughts and prayers. Always call me, if you need.

Love, Dad

I appreciated that the letter from my father was included in the church program. Even though I had such a hard time with them, I realized that they were doing their best to raise their sons well. Their religious beliefs had substantial issues and caused damage to Darin and me, but they did and do love their children and tried to do right by us.

We were treated with a musical number that took me by surprise and brought the entire congregation to tears. A Christian band called MercyMe, which I'd never heard of, sang a song called "I Can Only Imagine."

I can only imagine what it will be like
When I walk by Your side
I can only imagine what my eyes will see
When Your face is before me
I can only imagine
Surrounded by Your glory
What will my heart feel
Will I dance for You, Jesus
Or in awe of You be still
Will I stand in Your presence
Or to my knees will I fall
Will I sing hallelujah
Will I be able to speak at all
I can only imagine

This song has become very near and dear to my heart. Every time I required my brother's comfort, the song would just come on—from a playlist, the radio, wherever, in the most unheard-of situations. I always knew he was watching down and guiding me in my life's decisions. Whenever I hear this song, I know I'm able to communicate spirit to spirit with my brother with the understanding that I am making the right choice.

Darin's final resting place is out on the edge of a small town in rural Connecticut on a hill overlooking a field of flowers in the spring and the beautiful New England colors in the fall. As we buried him, the anchor in my life was gone and I was set adrift.

Chapter 4

Looking for Love

Humpty Dumpty sat on a wall,
Humpty Dumpty had a great fall.
All the king's horses and all the king's men
Couldn't put Humpty together again.

People have forever asked me the same question, "Why are you single? You have so much to offer. You're really a terrific catch because you have integrity, own a great home, have a wonderful job and a nice car, and can offer someone stability."

My response is always, "The good ones are all taken."

I have been on many dates, have subjected myself to the whole online dating scene, and have been involved in several relationships. Nothing ever lasted very long. My track record in love has been less than stellar.

After I came out on national television during my junior year of high school, I figured that I might as well jump into pursuing a relationship with the people I wanted to date rather than continuing to pretend with girls. The emotional barriers within my family prevented me from drawing significant emotional support from my parents, and my school certainly was not helpful to me. So I looked for personal fulfillment in romance.

My first relationship was with a guy who lived three thousand miles away on the West Coast. I was young and naïve and fell for someone a few years older. I learned important things from that relationship, like how vital it is to be safe in any kind of intimacy and to be aware of how men could take advantage of my innocence. I eventually ended the relationship due to the long distance. I needed more than a rendezvous every few months.

It was at least two years before I pursued another relationship. I had just started a new job, and the man who interviewed and hired me was very debonair and intriguing. He was a former recruiter for the United States Air Force, which meant he had to appear to be very straight to survive in that environment. Any suspicion of homosexuality would lead to an immediate dishonorable discharge. I found his straight appearance very attractive but kept my distance because I actually had no clue that he was gay until he invited me out on a date.

We hit it off from the start. We spent all of our time together and took day trips to Boston and New York City, and he eventually invited me to go with him to Disney World for a two-week vacation. Shortly after that trip, he asked me to move in with him, and we spent the next three years together.

The first two years were wonderful, but during our third year, he started to distance himself from me—emotionally and physically. The cold detachment was almost unbearable because it was such a drastic change. Then he told me something that completely blindsided me— he had to break off our relationship. I asked if he was seeing someone else, and he said no, absolutely not—only for me to find out that one of my good female friends was already four months pregnant with his child. I felt as if a hammer had hit me in the skull.

In a tail spin, I left our home. Darin arranged for my parents to allow me to move back into my childhood bedroom. I had always worked to maintain my relationship with my parents, but this was the first time I'd lived in their home since I'd become emancipated at sixteen. It provided a more firm reconciliation with them, which I was grateful for.

While staying temporarily with my parents, I experienced two different but parallel lives. I didn't hide anything from anyone, but I could not allow my family life to overlap with my love life. My parents continued to reiterate that they believed that I had chosen a gay "lifestyle" and that homosexual relationships were immoral. I didn't want to start another fight, so I kept the two parts of my life completely separate. My parents did not meet my dates, and my dates did not meet my family. However, I was still suffering from the heartache of losing the only man I had ever lived with and who I cared for very much. Because the two distinct parts of my life had no crossover, I dealt with this heartache alone.

I spent the next two years avoiding any hint of romance. The hurt was too deep to allow me to fall into the same hole again. I continued to pursue my career and eventually became a regional manager for a large cosmetics firm whose products were sold in high-end department stores. I covered most of New England and had nine accounts within the Connecticut market. One day, we were having a ribbon-cutting ceremony for a new store opening. The human resources manager for the department store started to flirt with me, and wow, was he my type to a T. He looked like he'd walked off the cover of *GQ Magazine*.

Though Caden was closeted and wanted no one to know about his homosexuality, we developed a deepening bond that I thought was going to last forever. The first time he invited me on a date, he suggested that we could play pool and grab a beer. I enthusiastically accepted, and we both quickly realized that neither of us played pool or drank beer. We cooked dinner together at his apartment instead.

Every time Caden made an advance—our first hug, our first kiss—he asked my permission. He didn't want to move fast, and it was a level of sweetness straight out of a romance novel. Our song was "Nothing Compares to You."

After eight months of bliss, I called him two days in a row but received no reply. When I was finally able to get him on the phone, he stated sharply that he was on the other line with his brother. I never heard from him again. He transferred to a different department store out of my territory and was gone. I was devastated.

A pattern for disaster was emerging in my love life, and I wondered what I was doing wrong. Did I attract flighty men who couldn't commit to a lifelong relationship? Was the gay community in general superficial and shallow in their relationships? I also wondered if this happened in the heterosexual world as well. It does, but seems to be more prevalent in our community possibly because of the lack of general social acceptance.

The heartbreak with Caden was much deeper than with the others—I truly loved him. The lack of closure made it even worse, and this time, my avoidance of another relationship lasted four years. I had my job and many friends, but the silence of my lonely house was deafening. A full ten years later, Caden found me on Google and contacted me to apologize profusely. He said that he had been in love with me but didn't know how to deal with it. His call was prompted because someone he had fallen in love with had abandoned him in the same way he had left me. He felt a heavy burden to express his regrets. I mustered the courage to ask if he was seeing anyone now. He was—someone who reminded him of me. "I think that's why I like him." I appreciated the relief of closure, but it generated another deep strain of disappointment.

My next attempt at dating was online. This was my introduction on Match.com:

> Here is where I try to appear witty and desirable to all you internet folks. Hopefully this whole essay will come together just like a 3 a.m. English paper you should have written last week. My perfect date would be adventurous with conservative undertones, whatever that means. (My mother always told me I wouldn't be taken seriously if I put out on the first date.) I'm looking for a cerebral connection as well as a physical one. I like fine dining and love to get together with friends over wine rather than a huge keg party. Always searching for Shangri-la, I consider myself religious. Looking for someone who can appreciate life! My interests: Doing what someone says can't be done, enjoying nature, entertaining, and most of all, day trading stocks online is my only addiction.

Within twenty-four hours, I was overwhelmed with eighteen e-mails saying the same thing: "Your profile is so amazing. Where have you been my whole life?" I was so ecstatic that I replied back to everyone. My excitement was short-lived. I received only one second response.

When Alan and I met for the first time in person, it was love at first sight. We dated for a while but we lived two hours apart, and the relationship faded as geographical distance became an issue. He was unhappy with his surroundings but not willing to make a change. I also busted him surfing a gay dating website and broke up with him two days before we were to leave for a vacation in San Diego. I decided to go on the trip with him anyway because we were using my frequent flier miles, but that was a mistake. The week was supposed to be heaven. Instead it was pure torture. When we returned, we parted ways—forever, I thought.

He resurfaced in my life as the funeral director for my brother's memorial service and was exceedingly supportive. I appreciated extra access to the funeral home for my own private time to grieve, but I was startled when Alan came up behind me when I was weeping alone in the viewing room.

He wrapped his arms around me and started crying too. "I made the biggest mistake of my life, and I will forever regret the pain that I caused you. This past year, I would have done anything to get you back. I am so sorry. Can I do anything to make it up to you?"

I was trying to cope with my brother's death and *now* he brought up our former relationship? Even through the haze of my grieving, I could tell that I could have Alan back in a second. But breaking up had hurt too much the first time, and I wasn't willing to take another chance with him.

When my relationship with Alan ended, I decided to take a different tack. Normally, I would go into hibernation for years before pursuing another relationship. This time, my feelings of rejection were vented by immediately posting the same personal profile on multiple dating websites. I promptly met another man who lived several hours away. Like the others, he was tall and handsome, caring and kind. The distinct difference was that he was in the middle of a divorce. When he married a woman, he knew he was gay. He never acted on it, hoping that heterosexual marriage would prove satisfactory, but after nine years and two daughters, he knew he had to be honest with his wife. He never engaged in a relationship with a man until after he separated from his wife.

We enjoyed many weekends of cuddling, day trips, and all the wonderful things couples in love do. Not everything was great. I have a very outgoing and upbeat personality, and I speak to everyone I meet. He was tremendously insecure, so my gregarious socializing made him extremely jealous, and we fought often. He was forever apologizing and begging for another chance. I finally determined to end the relationship. The demise took place when we spent two weeks in Hawaii. After our plane landed in Boston, we did not speak for six months. What is it about me and vacations?

Again, I immediately posted a personal ad. One of my first responses was from a doctor. We had several conversations over the phone, and agreed to meet for dinner and cocktails. The next morning, I sent a flirty email.

"Doctor: what was your diagnosis of last night? My identification of symptoms is rapidly beating rhythms in my heart. Should I call my physician?" His reply was within minutes. "I thought about you this morning but didn't want to look like a stalker and call you so fast."

The chemistry between us was quick and easy, and we soon spent a phenomenal weekend in New York City. He was impressed with all the restaurants I knew and recommendations for places to go and kept joking that I would make the perfect doctor's wife.

We made plans for a summer holiday weekend, but as it approached, several days went by without him contacting me. I didn't think anything of it—being a doctor placed many extra demands on his time. But the designated weekend passed with no word, and a couple of days later, a friend called. "I saw your doctor boyfriend online, cruising a website for a date."

I was furious with this betrayal. I sent him an e-mail demanding an explanation. He left a voice mail simply saying that things were not working out and repeating, "I'm sorry. I'm really sorry."

This has been my history of relationships with gay men since I first came out as a teenager—always searching for love but never finding the commitment that I was so desperately seeking. I know that I am not alone in feeling this way. I was determined to continue the search for that special man who shared my desire for a long-term romance with the solid values of promising monogamy, maintaining faithfulness throughout our lives, becoming best friends and confidantes in everything, and helping to carry each other's burdens.

After visiting many dating websites and being propositioned by numerous married men in conservative suits, it amazed me how easy a surface, noncommittal, physically gratifying fling was to come by. And, conversely, how truly rare an emotionally fulfilling, committed, and loving relationship was in those places. These men hiding in "straight suits" fill the corporate world. Believe me, I know. And so many openly admitted to being married and were only looking for a casual encounter. It has continually baffled me. I have been betrayed by someone who I loved and who I thought loved me. It's devastating. At that time, I could never have even considered being involved with a married man. My morals simply did not allow it. I could not stomach thinking of the heartache my actions would cause his wife.

When the relationship with the doctor didn't develop into anything lasting, I was in my mid-thirties. I had a Mercedes and an architecturally fabulous condo with a stream out my window and Pottery Barn furniture laid out straight from a photo shoot. I traveled a lot for my job all over the country, took international vacations, and saw a lot of beautiful cities. I made excellent money.

I deliberately created a view of my life for others that everything was awesome. I used social media, conducted interviews as a lifestyle reporter on television, and was a social butterfly at events. I was very good at putting up the front that my life was perfect in every way, physically, emotionally, and spiritually. Everyone wanted to be like Dennis. That's all I heard when I ran into friends or people from my social media accounts: "I want your life!"

I didn't want my life. It looked great from the outside but it had no foundation—it was a baseless castle in the air. I had lost my brother the year before. I worked to maintain a cordial relationship with my parents, but they still had never accepted my sexual orientation and often warned me of my impending damnation and consignment to hellfire. Any kindness we managed came from opposite sides of an unspoken gulf that could not be bridged.

It is reasonable to also look for emotional stability and an anchor in a life partner, regardless of one's sexual orientation. But I was failing there too. It had been almost twenty years since my first relationship, and I had bounced from one to the next. I was descending into frantic desperation to find someone—anyone—to spend my life with.

My search for emotional and physical intimacy took a hard turn for the worse on a New Year's Day when I was setting goals. I was going to find someone that year, and I didn't care where. Feeling like I was out of more worthy options for the search, I registered on a less-than-desirable website. I titled my profile, "Adventurous with conservative undertones, always searching for Shangri-La."

As usual, I was bombarded with explicit responses. For these people, it is a game, a rush. I was appalled at what I found. I was looking for someone who would be faithful, honest, and sincere. Was that too much to ask? On these websites, obviously yes, but I was feeling low enough to take a shot into the dark.

Searching for love in the wrong places can have disastrous results no matter your orientation. I felt I was getting older, less desirable. My resolution to avoid men who were already in a committed relationship collapsed under the weight of my loneliness, and I was willing to compromise my principles for a chance at happiness. The man of my dreams appeared on the horizon. His name was Byron, and he was married.

Compelled by curiosity and desperation, I crossed into the forbidden zone. I agreed to meet him for coffee. We connected right from the start and the conversation flowed as if we'd known each other for years. I asked the most important question first.

"Why are we meeting? What do you want from me?" I explained, "I usually don't put myself in compromising situations. I've never knowingly met someone for a date who is married. Does your wife know? Do you have an open relationship?"

He put his hand over his heart. "No, she doesn't know, and we don't have an open relationship. I just want friends to do things with, like hiking, kayaking, watching movies together, laughing."

I wasn't sure what to make of that so I asked him bluntly if he's gay or straight.

"I am most definitely gay!"

"So why are you married?"

He was sure of his answer, as if he'd justified it to himself hundreds of times through the years. "My wife and I have been married fourteen years, but if things had been different then, I never would have gotten married." He paused, looking uncomfortable. "Now I feel like I'm stuck."

I wasn't sure whether to believe him, but he went through an explanation of wanting to separate from his wife, but her mother had become ill and passed away, so he stayed. He had dated another man without telling his wife, and they fell in love. When he was given the ultimatum to leave his wife, he broke things off. He regretted that because he knew true love is hard to find, and he vowed to never make that mistake again.

Our talk turned to our careers, and we realized that we had actually met briefly about five years earlier. He had stopped at a hair salon to get a haircut at the same time I was there for a sales appointment. He was so suave and sophisticated. I am normally very professional in my business interactions, but I just couldn't help myself. This stranger and I flirted and laughed together, and then he walked away. Byron said he had wondered occasionally where I lived and if I was dating anyone.

Now we were sitting together in a coffee shop, meeting for a date after connecting online. Coincidence? Fate? We came to the conclusion that we'd had such a powerful impact on each other that it left an impression that lasted for years. I immediately thought that this could definitely progress into a fulfilling relationship.

As I left the date later that afternoon, I was ecstatic. But my mind started swirling as my morals tried to fight their way to the surface of the whirlpool of thoughts.

Am I setting myself up for failure? What the heck am I doing? He's married! He's emotionally unavailable. I can't allow myself to get involved with somebody like that. I'm going to be the third person, the one who always comes last. Every night he will go home and fall asleep next to her, not me.

This is not morally right. This is not what I stand for. I have values. I could never hurt anyone, and I don't want his wife to ever find out about me going on a date with her husband. I have to end it.

That pulled me up short. What was there to end? It hadn't even started.

My loneliness stepped up to the plate. *Yes, it has! It started five years ago!*

My conscience pushed back. *Why am I having these feelings of love for someone I just met for a couple of hours? Am I that desperate? Do I need therapy? I'm an independent person. I've lived alone most of my life, and I don't need anybody to fill a space in my home, especially not someone who is already committed to another person.*

My common sense and morals told me I could lose my heart, my dignity and pride, and my reputation. But logic isn't always in control. I had been so lonely for so long and felt like I had tried everything else. Byron and I had connected so well. He was already on the verge of separating from his wife. He didn't want a fling. He wanted a companion.

By the time I got home, I made my decision. *I will explore this! I owe it to myself to take a chance at finding a long-term relationship.*

I truly believed that fate had brought us together, and he was the soulmate I had been looking for all my life. But I had placed myself directly into the vortex of an affair and being the Other Man.

It was a seven-month roller coaster of intense emotions, including an immense amount of guilt that I was interfering with and breaking the true sanctity of a marriage. Byron made many promises that he was going to leave his wife to partner with me, but when he finally did separate from her, it was long after I had left the picture. I ended the relationship for my own emotional and mental well-being.

During this time, I wrote a fairly extensive journal to justify my misdeeds to myself and showed it to a friend. She wanted to publish it, including emails between Byron and me, as a memoir, and Byron was fully supportive. It quickly became a best seller, but as soon as it did, I was extremely embarrassed that my inner life was out there on paper. All the world could see that I was the Other Man, the person who had an affair with a married man.

The day I felt most insecure was when I was giving a speech at my local library. My high school typing teacher attended and wanted to purchase an autographed copy of my book. She was so proud that one of her students had become a published author! I wanted to crawl under the table and dissolve into the carpet. I was horribly mortified that she would come across explicit scenes, and I wanted to pretend that she wasn't going to read it. Oh, did I feel shame and guilt! I definitely did not feel like a good Christian man with moral beliefs and high standards. I was instead advancing the awful and incorrect stereotype that LGBT people are uncommitted and promiscuous.

Chapter 5

Reset Button on Life

This above all: to thine own self be true
And it must follow, as the night the day
Thou canst not then be false to any man.

~ *Hamlet*, act I, scene iii, lines 78–80

I am many things. I am a people person, a talker, a networker. I am a gay man, a survivor of a hate crime, an advocate for the LGBT community. I am a friend, a hugger, a Christian who has always believed in Heavenly Father and Jesus Christ. I am a son, a brother, a cousin. All of this and more collectively defines who and what I am.

I am unashamed of who I am, and I am proud of what I have done and what I have overcome. But despite the outward appearance of a rewarding and happy life, there was a gaping chasm in my heart that was caused by first losing my parents' love and support because of my sexual orientation, then losing my brother to his drug addiction, and finally, losing my own connection to God because of my poor choices.

Even in my darkest times, I still believed in the faith that I learned alongside Katie as little children at the Congregational church. I remembered how loved we were and how close to God I felt then. Oh, how I wanted to have that again. But because of the affair with Byron, I knew that I had crossed a major line and dug myself into a spiritual hole that was going to take a very, very long time to climb out of. It didn't matter why I had done it. I knew it was wrong, and there was no excusing it. It had put me so far from God that I didn't even know which direction to go.

So I did the only thing I could think of. I started putting a lot of time and energy into helping other people. I thought that even if it didn't help me, at least I could make someone else's day better and brighten the dark night of the soul.

I volunteered a lot in various capacities. I've always believed in service, and giving back to my community provided a little of the peace and happiness I was looking for. Those were some very difficult years in all areas of my life, including absorbing some serious financial blows during the global stock market crash in 2008. But my service was rewarding, and the joy it brought carried through my own trying times. It made me focus on building a better world for others even when my own wasn't that great. The best part was that I realized I had found my path back to God. I knew it was going to be very long and that I was probably going to be lonely at times, but I could finally say to myself that I had started my journey home.

It was time to hit the reset button on life in general. I was tired of all the traveling I had to do for my job, and wanted to find something that would let me work from home. I was still lonely and looking for emotional security, but I had given up on finding a compatible life partner who shared my beliefs and values to provide that stability. I wasn't dating or even looking for dates. Instead, I wanted a quiet sanctuary to rediscover God and uplift my soul. I wanted a place that would provide a safe harbor to shelter in during the storms of life. I had always felt a pull toward faith and religion, so after more than twenty years, I was ready to go back to church.

I was not comfortable returning to the Congregational church so close to my parents' home, so I started church hopping. Every week, I visited a different denomination—Baptist, Catholic, Episcopalian, Lutheran, Congregational, any little church that said they believed in Jesus Christ. I attended churches where no one knew me, and I made sure to not be noticed. This was the opposite of my professional career in front of a camera as a network marketer and TV host, but I did not want a lot of attention within a church. I just wanted a religious home where I could sit quietly to rebuild and replenish my spirit for the week ahead.

What were my qualifications for choosing a church? I believe that Jesus Christ is the Son of God who died for our sins, so the first requirement was that it be Christian with teachings from the Bible. Almost as important, I wanted a church family that would not try to change who God made me to be—and that is a 100 percent gay man. As a member of the LGBT community, I found it difficult to find a church that I really connected with. Don't get me wrong. Many churches are accepting, especially nowadays, of gays and lesbians. It was encouraging to see how much had changed in my community in the many years since I was attacked at my high school. But as I visited various churches, I didn't feel an emotional or spiritual connection with any of them. The people were always warm and welcoming. The sermons were always from the Bible and shared the teachings of Jesus and the prophets. The ministers and pastors told us to be kind and love our neighbors. Maybe that would have been sufficient when I was a teenager or young adult. But now, as a grown man desperately trying to find God again, it wasn't enough. I wanted more.

I wanted a place that would plant me firmly in gospel soil and water the seed of my faith. I wanted a church that would not only nourish me with the good word of God but also help me grow into the man of God I wanted to become. I wanted to find a cocoon for my spiritual rebirth, a renewal that would finally fill that cavity in my soul. I wanted a spiritual home. As a believer in God and Christ, I felt that such a church was somewhere out there, but I hadn't found it yet.

The only church I never stepped foot in was The Church of Jesus Christ of Latter-day Saints. The only thing I understood about Mormons was that they had the same reaction toward gays that my parents' church did—they believed gays were immoral and going to hell just for our orientation. I was not interested in another homophobic religious experience, thank you very much. I also thought that I wasn't allowed to attend even if I wanted to because I thought you had to be baptized in order to enter their church buildings. Maybe that's some work for their marketing department.

At the same time that I was looking for a new church, I was also looking for a new job. In May 2014, after many months of research into home-based businesses, I found an incredible ground-floor opportunity with a company that was starting to pick up momentum. Qivana was a multi-level marketing company that stood for everything I believe in relating to physical health: lessening people's dependency on pharmaceutical drugs by combining breakthrough science and research from doctors and Nobel Prize winners with third-party-tested natural products. I was more than a little anxious about quitting my old job and starting a new endeavor, but a quiet voice inside said that this was the right choice for me.

I took the leap of faith and signed up for the largest franchise package at $1,000. My first weekly paycheck was $1,400, my second was $800, my third was $1,600, and so on. By my fifth week, I had become a leader in the company by reaching a status level that got me noticed by the owners. The following week, I achieved another rank advancement for promotion by helping others achieve the same. I was making a difference in people's lives, and it was rewarding both emotionally and financially. I love helping people, and this job let me earn a good paycheck while doing that. It was the perfect career move for me.

Six months after joining the company, I participated in a conference call with all the owners. By the end of the call, I could tell they cared about us in the field. They made it clear we didn't work for them; they worked for us. It was December, a few days before Christmas, and somehow we started talking about attending church. I now knew they were Christian. I had no idea which church they affiliated with, but I didn't care. I knew that they cared about me personally. I wasn't Dennis the gay man. I wasn't Dennis the guy who didn't go to church. I wasn't even Dennis the guy from Connecticut. To them, I was *just Dennis*, and I loved it!

Early in my time with Qivana, I learned that many of my fellow coworkers belonged to The Church of Jesus Christ of Latter-day Saints. Prior to this, I had never met a member of the Church except for the poor missionaries who had my door repeatedly slammed in their faces. So I was shocked that my sexual identity didn't seem to bother these Mormons I worked with. I wondered if they even really *were* Mormon. So, at a conference, I nervously approached my friend Cheryl.

I said, "You're Mormon, right?"

"Yes, I am."

"I'm gay." I felt like I was making an announcement.

She didn't react. "I know."

I repeated myself. "You're a Mormon."

"Yeah."

"And I'm gay."

"Yeah."

I paused and studied her for a few seconds. My being gay didn't seem to bother her one bit. There was no lecture about choosing an immoral lifestyle, not even a facial expression of disdain. One more time. "You're a Mormon."

She took me by the shoulders. "It doesn't matter what you do or who you are. It isn't for me to judge. You're Dennis and you're my friend, and I love you as you are."

How can I describe the burden that was lifted from my soul? One of the hardest things about being gay is that you always worry someone is going to judge you or condemn you for being exactly as God made you. I knew that Mormons were conservative and traditional. I knew, or at least thought I knew, that gays weren't welcome in their faith. But Cheryl accepted me exactly as I am. Being gay is just one part of my identity. This is when I first realized that she saw me as just Dennis and that she accepted and loved all of me.

Okay then. That was not what I expected.

After that, I watched the company owners and their wives a little more closely. They made charitable contributions to many organizations and had integrity in conducting the business. They were honest in their dealings with us and their customers. They were always kind and supportive to me personally, even when I was sometimes risqué with what I posted on social media. They always edified me as a leader on the convention stage, at meetings, and on corporate conference calls. They never judged me for being a funny, openly gay, LGBT advocate. They were very good people, so maybe, even though they belonged to what I understood to be a homophobic church, they could provide some spiritual guidance and reassurance. I hadn't been able to find it anywhere else, so I figured I might as well talk to my coworkers and company leadership.

In September 2016, I mentioned this to Cheryl, and she suggested I talk to Shelby, the wife of one of the company owners. Shelby is an amazing person who I had previously connected with well, so about a month after seeing her at a convention, I called her.

"What can I do for you, Dennis?"

The first thing I said was, "I need to tell you I'm gay." I'm sure it's pretty obvious when people meet me, but I still feel like I need to confirm it.

"And?" Wow, that's the same non-reaction Cheryl had. My being gay didn't faze these Mormons one bit.

"I have to tell you, I'm looking for a home, a family religion. What I mean by that is a place to belong." I told her I wanted and needed God in my life but didn't know where to go. I talked about church hopping and visiting several congregations that said they accept gays, but I didn't feel like they truly did. I told her about my parents' extreme religious conversion when I was a teenager and how my mother looked me straight in the face so many times and said, "Jesus does not love you."

Shelby stopped me cold. "Hold it right there. Jesus *does* love you."

She said those four words with force, pausing after each one. With those four words, Shelby punched straight through decades of insecurity, fear, longing, isolation, and sadness. It was the first time since I was seventeen and came out as gay that I was told that Jesus loves me. No qualifiers. No behavior caveats. Just "Jesus loves you." That's it.

I immediately burst into tears.

She kept going. "God is not a respecter of persons. Jesus loves everyone, including you." As I sobbed years of heartache into the phone, she reassured me over and over that God loves me just the way I am. He just does. In that one crystalizing moment, the God-shaped hole in my heart began to fill. I felt a love that I hadn't felt in many years that I can only describe as divine. I kept crying, but my tears were becoming tears of joy in hearing that God really did love me, a 100 percent gay man. I didn't have to change who I am one bit. He loves me the same as anyone else and accepts me exactly as He made me.

I eventually confirmed that Shelby belongs to The Church of Jesus Christ of Latter-day Saints and asked her straight out if a gay person could become a member of the Church. "Absolutely."

"But there are rules?"

"You can join the Church as long as you're not in a same-sex relationship."

Quite frankly, this did not bother me a bit right then, and I blew it off. "Well, I'm not, and I haven't been for a while." I had Shelby validating that God accepts me as I am. What else was there?

Shelby and I talked often over the next few months, probably weekly. I called her with any question or problem that I wanted or needed help with. She was, and continues to be, my personal guardian angel guiding me on my path back to my heavenly home. Sometimes she would put her husband, Derek, on the phone to answer my question if she thought he could explain something better. The first few conversations were continual reassurance that she and God accept my sexual orientation and background—I had a hard time wrapping my mind around this acceptance because I'd been so conditioned to believe otherwise. Slowly, their love broke through my doubts, fears, and skepticism, and I began to understand what Shelby so powerfully believes.

I started asking questions about the Church. Shelby had Andrew, another person with the company who I already knew, follow up with me to answer a lot of my questions and help point me to resources to learn more about the Church. Andrew helped me download a number of apps for my phone of scriptures, commentaries, inspirational videos, and other things. He occasionally sent me specific links on LDS.org that he thought I would find interesting.

Shelby and Andrew also both invited me to watch general conference during the first weekend in October, a semiannual broadcast from Salt Lake City to hear the Church leaders speak. I didn't understand much of it—the verbiage of talking about certain angels and prophets within the Book of Mormon, like Nephi and Moroni, was unfamiliar to me. However, that didn't stop me from feeling privileged to be welcomed more fully into their world, and I respected the uplifting messages presented. I still had many questions, but I started to realize how wrong I'd been about the Latter-day Saints. If you had asked me a year before if I thought that the Mormons would be the one church that would accept me as a gay man, I would have said that you were nuts. But here I was, and they loved and accepted me as I am.

All of my learning about the Church was on the phone or online with Shelby and Andrew. I didn't know any members in Connecticut, so I had no one to talk to in person. Sometimes, when I had a question about the Church and didn't feel like bothering them with another phone call, I would go to Barnes & Noble to look for books about the Mormons and people who had converted and been baptized. Much to my disappointment, the Barnes & Noble stores on the East Coast do not carry any books about the Mormon faith. I was surprised, considering they have a large religious section with representation from all over Christianity including Catholicism, Billy Graham, evangelical, Amish, Joel Osteen, Devotional Bibles, study Bibles, and dozens of other versions of the Bible. But there was nothing about the Book of Mormon or Joseph Smith. That was frustrating.

At the same time I was beginning this major faith transition, work had a major evolution as well. In March 2017, Qivana merged with a company called Zija. It was one of the best things that could have happened as well as the one of the scariest. The fear of losing the Qivana identity contrasted with the excitement of gaining pharmaceutical-grade essential oils and a plethora of related products. As a company leader at Qivana and an essential oil expert, I was flown out to Lehi, Utah, a couple of months later to tour the corporate office, meet the new executives, visit with the doctors and scientists, and see the shipping facility and manufacturing plant.

After all of the online and phone conversations with Andrew, it was really nice to see him in person on this trip. He pulled me aside to share that he and his wife were planning a vacation to upstate New York to visit one of Joseph Smith's homes along with some other sacred and historic sites. He had discussed it with his wife, and they wanted to extend an invitation for me to join them on their trip so I could learn firsthand about the Church and its history.

What? Go on vacation with them? Who the heck is this guy? I'd known Andrew for years since he was always our go-to liaison for all the leaders in our company, and we had become friends, but I never expected to be invited on his personal vacation. This was definitely weird! Why would a straight Mormon guy who was young enough to be my son invite me on vacation with his wife? Despite my initial misgivings, I did feel flattered and privileged to be included, so I agreed to go.

I was staying at a Marriott hotel on this work trip. From my years of corporate traveling, I knew very well that all Marriott hotels have a Bible and a copy of the Book of Mormon in the desk of each room. Do you think in any of those hundreds of nights in a Marriott, I had ever opened a Book of Mormon? Of course not! Why would I? I knew that Mormons weren't going to accept me as a gay man, so why should I read their religious books? As I was packing to check out of the hotel, I opened a drawer to clear it of my belongings and saw a Book of Mormon there as well. Almost like a reflex and with no thought at all, it went into my bag along with everything else.

On my way home from Utah, I found a large group of missionaries at the gate waiting for the same flight I was on. They were going from the Missionary Training Center to their assigned mission area in Ohio. This was the first time I had actually met and talked to missionaries. As part of our introduction, I pulled the hotel's Book of Mormon out of my bag and showed them I had a copy. Right then, it occurred to me—I had just *stolen* that book of scripture! I said that to the missionaries, who found the situation hilarious. They laughed and laughed, and assured me that's why it was in the hotel in the first

Flying home from Utah with the missionaries

place—to be taken and read. I later found out that a former CEO of the Marriott Corporation often joked that he was the largest distributor of the Book of Mormon.

We talked on the entire flight about the Book of Mormon and what they do every day as missionaries. At the Detroit airport, I went with them to their next gate, where we had a prayer together and felt God's love for all of us. I didn't realize what it was at the time, but I felt so happy and connected with them. I was beginning to find my church home, and I didn't even know it.

Back in Connecticut, I was suddenly conflicted about going to visit Mormon historical sites with Andrew and his wife. I kept asking myself, *Dennis, are you nuts? Why are you wasting your time and money to go on vacation with someone you only know on a business level? Who goes on vacation to Mormon historical sites in the middle of nowhere New York anyway?* I felt some pressure, as if I were headed to a convention and would be pushed into signing on to the company right then and there. I tried to find excuses to cancel—I have family obligations, I have a business meeting I'm conducting, and so on.

But at the same time, there was a sense of peace that I really couldn't explain, like everything was going to be fine. It was a quiet feeling like the one that inspired me to join Qivana, not the loud, emotional pulsations of my parents' church. It was just a calm reassurance that God hadn't forgotten me and that He was guiding my feet along the path He wanted me to walk. Some of my worries began to melt away as I felt accepted and included in a way that I had not experienced in quite some time from anyone, including my own family. Darin was really the last person who made me feel that way. As it got closer to the trip date, Andrew and I talked on the phone more frequently so he could tell me about the places we would be visiting, and he often said how excited they were to introduce me to the Church's history.

My last ditch effort to get out of the trip was that I delayed booking my hotel reservation in anticipation that they would be sold out for that weekend. When I did call at the last minute, the hotel had one room left. Oh my goodness. I reserved it, and I was going.

I stepped up my research into the Church, which is the exact opposite of what I tell people to do when investigating a business opportunity. I strongly encourage potential business partners *not* to become a Google specialist. They should ask a lawyer, accountant, or other successful person about joining an MLM company rather than finding random things on the internet. Well, that didn't stop me from Googling The Church of Jesus Christ and their views on LGBT challenges.

What I found was extremely threatening and scary enough to make me want to run for the hills. All the stories, all the videos were nothing but disappointment, despair, and sadness. People were excommunicated from their church and disowned by their families and friends just for being gay and wanting to have a romantic relationship with another gay person. Far too often, this led to them ending their lives through suicide. Reading all of this distress sparked a lot of negative emotion and brought back disturbing memories of past interactions with my parents and their pastor forcefully shoving their beliefs onto me.

Why didn't I bail? That's a good question that I'm still unable to fully answer. Maybe now that I'm older and more experienced in dealing with this type of opposition, I have the strength to stand up against it when I see it against others or when it happens again in my own life. I do know that something inside kept pulling me forward and wanting to learn more. No matter what I read or saw online, I kept returning to a feeling of calm and quiet reassurance that God was with me. I was still going in the right direction, and I just had to keep putting one foot in front of another, walking by faith and not by sight. I didn't have any answers at this point, but I had hope.

Shelby reassured me in every single phone conversation that God loved me and that the members of the Church would accept me as I am as fully as she did. In every phone call, every text, every time we communicated, I felt God's love for me through her. Even though I was still scared of what I had read, it seemed like God was speaking to me with her voice. "Jesus *does* love you."

Chapter 6

They're Nuts. I Don't Want to Go to Palmyra!

Surround yourself with only people who
are going to lift you higher.[4]

~ Oprah Winfrey

On a hot Monday morning in July, I drove west for five and a half hours to meet Andrew and his wife, Audrey, in Susquehanna, Pennsylvania, out in the middle of nowhere at a place called the Priesthood Restoration Site. I had no clue what that meant, just that it was somehow important to the Mormons.

I was still quite nervous about going to all these sacred sites with Andrew and Audrey, so to gain reassurance, I called my coworker and friend Cheryl, who had been the first person in our business I had confirmed as being Mormon. I told her where I was going and asked her to keep the reason confidential. I frequently post many pictures on social media, and there would be some of this trip, but I wasn't ready to tell the world that I was actually intending to learn about the Mormon faith. She was very excited in my behalf.

"My husband and I were there last week and had a blast! You're going to love it. I'm thrilled you're going!"

I thought, *Well, I'm glad someone is!* I still was not so thrilled about it. I shared my hesitation and nervousness about the lack of understanding that the Church has for the LGBT community.

Cheryl went straight to the heart of it. "I'll be simple. When we hang up the phone after talking, I want you to pray to our Heavenly Father for a revelation, a message, a sign from God, the Holy Ghost, and Jesus Christ. He will lead you in the right direction. No doubt!"

So I did. I very bluntly asked God for a lot of things. *Please give me a sign that I'm making the right choice to possibly join the LDS Church. I need to know. Please don't let me be pressured by my friends to join before I'm ready. Are they going accept me for me? Am I making the biggest mistake of my life? I need to know if this is the right thing, and a good thing, or if I'm screwing something up.* I used a lot of non-LDS words and was very boisterous to God and spilled the deepest part of my soul out of my mouth. Then a very abrupt *Amen* to close. Nothing else.

I didn't expect a lightning bolt or a tornado to appear in the clear blue sky. I couldn't even imagine what "a sign" would be, so after a couple of minutes of quiet, I turned on my iTunes. Go figure. I was out in the middle of nowhere with no service. So I turned on the old-fashioned radio and hit Seek to find a station.

The signal search landed on a Christian radio station. *Oh, that's nice, let's listen to this.* The next song to begin playing was . . .

"I Can Only Imagine," by MercyMe.

The song from my brother Darin's funeral. The song I heard every time I felt like I was communicating with him from the next life. The song I heard every time I needed spiritual support and comfort. Could God have possibly worked any faster?

When the song reached the line, "Will I dance with you, Jesus," I lost it. The tears were flowing as if Niagara Falls had collapsed, the car filled up with steam, I couldn't see at all . . . and I was still driving on a major interstate. My body got tingly and the hair on my neck, arms, back, and entire body stood up. I could feel my brother's presence along with several others. Goodness, for all I knew I had Moroni, Nephi, Christ, God, and the entire Book of Mormon in my car offering soothing comfort and reassurance. I could almost smell Darin's cologne thirteen years after his passing.

Twenty minutes went by, and I still couldn't stop sobbing. So what do I do when my face is all red and my eyes are bloodshot and puffy from crying? I took a selfie!

I must have been swerving because I was pulled over by the state police. When the officer approached my window, I was still crying like a little baby and hyperventilating. He probably thought I was a nutcase with my babbling, but I managed to explain that I was missing my deceased brother and had just heard the song from his memorial service. Much to my surprise, he let me go.

Since I was parked on the side of the road anyway, I needed to do a little bit of communication. My phone signal worked enough for me to call Cheryl back and thank her for the encouragement to pray. I also called Shelby, because, well, I always called Shelby. I explained in detail what had just occurred, and she was overjoyed.

"I always knew you would experience something like this! What an incredible feeling to sense your brother's presence with Heavenly Father telling you that this is the path you need to take."

When I finally started driving again, it was another hour and a half to reach the Priesthood Restoration Site. I arrived there before Andrew and Audrey and was able to tour the visitors' center with the senior missionaries assigned there. I had no idea where I was and didn't understand the significance at all. I didn't have any moments of intense connection like I did in my car, but it was very peaceful, and I felt like I could sense the presence of God.

Now that I've been a member of the Church for a while, I've figured it out. Briefly, The Church of Jesus Christ of Latter-day Saints teaches that the priesthood authority given to the biblical Twelve Apostles by Jesus Christ during His mortal life was removed from the earth when those Apostles were all killed. We believe that in 1829, John the Baptist and Peter, James, and John from the Bible appeared to Joseph Smith and his assistant Oliver Cowdery as angels somewhere at this location in Pennsylvania (there's no marker that says "at this exact spot") and bestowed God's priesthood authority on them.

When Andrew and Audrey arrived, I was finally able to meet her for the first time and she gave me a hug. "I've heard about you for so long. It's great to finally meet you in person!"

We didn't stay much longer because Andrew said we had more places to visit. Suddenly it was as if the forces of nature were against us. The torrential rain was so intense that there were immediate flash-flood warnings. We drove as quickly as we could back to the main highway on roads threatened with being washed out.

We drove another two hours into eastern New York—wow, these Mormon sites are far apart—and ended up at a place with a sign that said "Peter Whitmer Farm." There was another visitors' center and a replica of a very small cabin. This is where The Church of Jesus Christ of Latter-day Saints was formally organized on April 6, 1830.

My mind was spinning with overload, so I didn't absorb much. I said very little, but I was listening. And feeling a lot. In the visitors' center, we went into a little glass room to watch a video. It was very short, but even that little bit made me cry. I had no idea why I was crying. In fact, I even said to myself, *Why am I crying? I'm not a crier. What is going on?* I was feeling the Spirit but didn't understand that yet.

Location number three was the big one—Palmyra, New York, with the Sacred Grove. We pulled into the parking lot of a beautiful 1800s-era farm with glistening trails like something out of a fairy tale. The day was hot and sunny with no clouds at all, and by this time, it was late afternoon. We went down the trail slowly, taking our time to enjoy nature and the silence. The trees were tall, and the sun beamed through the leaves with rays of light periodically illuminating the path.

When I had first been introduced to Audrey earlier in the day, she was difficult for me to read. I had this feeling that I was intruding and that she didn't understand why her husband's work acquaintance was here on vacation with them. Truthfully, I was wondering the same thing. It wasn't until here at the Sacred Grove that I felt we both connected. Andrew noticed a bench on a slight embankment off the trail and suggested that we sit down so they could explain more about where we were and about their church.

The story was all messed up in my head at the time, but now I have it straightened out. This is where Joseph Smith lived with his family when he was a teenager. There was a massive religious revival in the area with many competing churches, and Joseph's family split in two different directions. He wanted to join a church but was confused about which one was true, so he mainly just read the Bible. He found a verse that encouraged him to pray and ask God what he should

Dennis with Andrew and Audrey at the Sacred Grove

do—James 1:5 in the New Testament: "If any of you lack wisdom, let him ask of God." One day, he went to the woods, where we were, and prayed. Heavenly Father and Jesus Christ appeared to him and told him to join no church at that time. This is known as the First Vision.

We also talked a lot about "the Gospel Principles" and "the Plan of Salvation." I didn't understand anything. I wasn't committed to joining the Church. I was very confused. But I also didn't feel uncomfortable at all. There was a sense of peace over my entire body, and I had a strong desire to learn everything I could as fast as possible. Obviously, I can't learn the entire gospel in forty-eight hours, but I sure wanted to try!

I had a feeling like someone had given me a Valium, which absolutely did not occur, but I definitely felt the Spirit, a presence, maybe my brother watching over me. Andrew told me much, much later that they had prepared ahead of time and fully intended to give me the first missionary lesson in the Sacred Grove—I was there to learn, and they were going to teach me. I was going to know why that grove of trees is so special.

A major doubt was still unsettled: *They're going to want me to be baptized tonight, sign over my life to the Church, become straight, marry a woman, have children, and convert all my friends.* This had happened when my parents converted to the Pentecostal church, and I had never had any other experience learning about a church. It was all I knew, so I was afraid it would happen again.

We decided to leave that glorious patch of trees so we could tour the farmhouses. We were greeted by a missionary, Sister Guimaras. She took us into the first house, which is a small cabin, and the hair on my neck stood up and my entire body got goosebumps. I've always felt like I could get spiritual impressions, but not knowing what else to call it, I just referred to it as being psychic. Now I know that the Church believes in spiritual promptings and revelations. Anyway, this place felt very dark and frightening, like someone had died there.

I said rather suddenly, "Who was persecuted here? I feel like something bad happened here." Andrew and Audrey looked at me oddly, and I was suddenly afraid they were going to ask me to just get in my car and leave because I was being too weird.

The sister turned to them. "Does he know where he is?"

They shook their heads. "Not really. We've taken him to so many places just today."

I still didn't understand anything that had happened the entire day—where we had been, where we were, or what the history was for any of these places. It was all very overwhelming. But I did learn that this home was where Joseph Smith, the first leader of the Mormon Church, lived with his family when he was a teenager.

What really made me resonate with Joseph Smith is that he was a victim of many hate crimes, like I had been during high school, like Jesus Christ at His crucifixion, like many people of the LGBT community, and even like many members of the Church. He was beat up multiple times. He was tarred and feathered in the middle of the winter and left outside to freeze. He was wrongfully imprisoned many times. He was eventually shot and killed.

Sister Guimaras and I stepped out onto the back porch of the cabin where we could see the Sacred Grove, and she told me about Joseph Smith's vision, the same story Andrew and Audrey had talked about when we were out among the trees. She was so sincere in her words. I could tell that she fully believed that Heavenly Father and

Jesus Christ appeared to Joseph Smith, and that They love all people. As she spoke, I could feel God's love for me through the Holy Ghost, and yet again that day, I cried. I watched the sunset over the Sacred Grove while she told me that God loves me and I felt it. I knew what it was. It was the same overwhelming feeling of love that I felt the previous fall when Shelby and I spoke on the phone.

Shelby told me that God loves me. Sister Guimaras told me that God loves me. And standing on that porch, *God* told me that He loves me.

After the driving around and touring all day, the sites were closing for the night and it was time to head for the hotel. Alone in my room, I started reading the Book of Mormon from the beginning. I had previously read verses that Shelby and Andrew suggested to me, but it was time to read it all. I had felt the presence of the Holy Ghost and Heavenly Father, and I could no longer ignore the Book of Mormon and its testimony of Jesus Christ. It promised to fill a gap that had been open for a long time and provide the emotional stability I had been craving my entire adult life. I read until my eyes burned and I couldn't keep them open any longer.

The next morning, we drove a couple of hours to see Niagara Falls. I was tired from very little sleep but excited at the same time—the drive gave us some much-needed private time to talk about my concerns with the Church. I even had a list of questions on my iPad. I prefaced my questions by asking Andrew and Audrey to be completely open and honest with me in their answers and that I would not take offense to anything they said. I wanted to hear nothing but the truth about their experiences and lives as members of the church.

What caused you to be interested in Mormonism?

Andrew was ready with an answer: "Although we were both born into the Church, everyone is encouraged to gain a testimony of their own. We do not continue in the Church simply because our parents raised us this way. We have each discovered and developed our own faith."

What makes you think Joseph Smith was a true prophet of God and not Jesus?

This question makes me laugh now. I was trying to figure out why Joseph Smith came along so late in the game. Why did it take until the 1800s for the Latter-day Saint faith to start? I genuinely thought Joseph Smith was a new version of Jesus Christ Himself. He's not. He doesn't replace Jesus Christ at all. He's a spokesman for Christ, like Moses, Isaiah, Peter, Paul, and the rest of the Biblical prophets. Andrew and Audrey explained that Jesus Christ and Joseph Smith are two different people with two different roles.

What do you like about Mormons or the Mormon religion?

"It's like a family—there's camaraderie. We have friends throughout the world who are LDS. I have the presence of the Holy Ghost in my life. I appreciate the fact that I am sealed to my wife and family for eternity along with my ancestors and other relatives."

Do you have any concerns about the Mormon faith or areas you are not totally comfortable with?

"We may not always understand what the prophet is saying, but it's okay to ask questions to better understand. We have faith in Jesus Christ and that things will all work out eventually."

Personally, what's your view on gay marriage?

Andrew hesitated slightly, then said, "We believe that marriage is only between a man and a woman."

When I heard this, I was silent. His answer seemed extremely stern and abrupt to me, and quite frankly, not what I expected from two people in their twenties. I had figured they would be more open-minded. My stomach tightened into a knot, and I wondered if this church perhaps wasn't for me. I would never be with a man ever again. That's *it* . . . or I'd be excommunicated.

I didn't ask if they thought the Church would ever allow gay marriage in the future, because I was baffled by their naïveté and misunderstanding of the LGBT community. In the end, I was disappointed by their answers. I could be baptized into The Church of Jesus Christ even though I'm gay, but I would not be allowed to pursue a gay relationship in any way. I would have to deprive myself of physical and emotional romantic connection for the rest of my life. This was not a happy thought. I didn't want to spend my life alone and die as a single old man.

I already knew that the Mormon Church would not allow me to be in a same-sex relationship if I became a member. Shelby had told me that in the very first conversation months before. But they say that you need to hear something several times before you really get it. This was my moment when it hit—the choice I was going to have to make. Be a member of the Mormon Church as a forever-single person, or stay outside of it so I could search again for a man to share my life with.

Another question I asked in the course of conversation was how they could tell if someone was Mormon just from looking at them. Audrey explained that sometimes you notice a positive light about a person in their eyes or in their countenance and can just tell that there is something different about them. However, there are many other subtle things to watch for, including what people wear and how they speak. We talked about "alternate swears" like *darn, shoot, gosh, oh my heavens,* and *holy cow!* Andrew told me later that both he and Audrey were impressed as I immediately started to consciously change my language, and they realized, at that moment, that I had a sincere desire to explore this church further. Now, I know that it was the influence of the Holy Ghost helping me to be more respectful. Truthfully, I was still apprehensive about all of this, but I was serious about learning more. It was just something I felt compelled to do. I corrected myself from actual swears to the alternate words. I'd never been taught *not* to use bad words. My questionable language had been so habitual that I never noticed it until Andrew pointed it out. From that moment on, I didn't *want* to use bad language. I noticed it constantly and corrected myself instantly. That's not to say I don't still mess up occasionally— nobody's perfect. But when you are open to change, Heavenly Father can move mountains.

When we arrived at Niagara Falls, it was time to take a break from religious conversations. We spent the first half of the day enjoying the exhibits and attractions. If the day before hadn't been enough, this fully cemented my friendship with Andrew and Audrey. Fun times together are just as important to relationships as the more serious conversations. It was a huge source of satisfaction to revel in our playful sides together. I felt that they enjoyed my company as much as I liked theirs, and they weren't dragging me around out of some kind of obligation to be nice. We put on the funny-looking garbage-bag ponchos to stay dry on the boat going to the base of the falls, only to have humidity and water running in all directions. It was so hot and muggy, it felt like we were on the equator. I'd been to the falls before, but this time they seemed to be radiating beams of light shining from the heavens.

When we finished at Niagara, we headed back to Palmyra for more historic sites and an event. Who knew upstate New York had so much Mormon heritage? We stopped on top of a mountain to take some photos in front of a statue. It turns out this hill, called Cumorah, was where Joseph Smith dug up the gold plates that became the Book of Mormon, but I had no idea then. It was just some random hill. The statue, however, triggered a deep spiritual connection that I still can't explain. From the second I heard the name Moroni and realized this was a statue of him, I wanted to know everything I could about him. I'm very obsessed with everything Moroni: pictures, statues, books—even his image as a Church logo. This obsession is really unusual for me because I usually have such a hard time choosing favorites of anything. But there's something about Moroni that I resonate with as if he is my own personal guardian angel.

At the Hill Cumorah Visitors' Center, we saw Sister Guimaras from the Smith cabin. Because of our experience together the night before, I was drawn to her like a powerful magnet. We went into a room with an entire curving wall of windows and a Christus statue in the center. Sister Guimaras played a recording of Christ's words from the New Testament, and I wept yet again. It was the overwhelming presence of so many spirits—Darin, the Holy Ghost, maybe even Moroni! I didn't tell anyone because surely they would think I was crazy for talking to dead people. I was hypersensitive to all my surroundings. I was overwhelmed with all of the lessons and history. The overload of emotion was pouring out my eyes.

I saw that Andrew was taking pictures of Sister Guimaras and me speaking together, so I tried to compose myself and smile while focusing on what she was saying, but I couldn't quite pull it together to keep myself from tears. The actual photo captured my emotional struggle of containing the profound peace and joy I was feeling in that moment.

We next visited the historical printing press in Palmyra where the first copies of the Book of Mormon were created. All of the history is incredible. Even though I wasn't Mormon (yet), I respected all of the challenges, roadblocks, and tribulations that the Latter-day Saint community faced in the early 1800s and admired their resilience in overcoming them.

*Dennis speaking with Sister Guimaras at the
Hill Cumorah Visitors' Center*

We also walked around the outside of the Palmyra New York Temple, tucked into the trees at the top of a little hill near the Smith farm. I'd seen temples from a distance, but this was the first time I'd gone close to one and learned the difference between temples and regular church buildings. Audrey explained it while I filmed her, so I could listen to it again later and internalize what she had said. Once I had a better understanding of the differences between the two, I was *so* grateful that I had never started a protest during the open house of the Hartford Connecticut Temple.

When we went to the Hill Cumorah Pageant, I was told that there would be multiple protestors with large signs and megaphones, shouting over and over, "You're not of God! You don't believe in Jesus!"

As an LGBT advocate, I've been to many protests. This is right up my alley, so I was feeling comfortable about how to handle the situation. I was told that it's best to just walk by and ignore them, and *not* to draw attention to ourselves. That was excruciating because I wanted so much to protect my new friends. It's such a lie that the Latter-day Saint faith doesn't believe in Heavenly Father and Jesus Christ. There's a huge statue of Jesus Christ and many paintings about His life in the New Testament right near where those people were standing with their megaphones. How could I feel so much love from God and the Saints if they didn't believe in Jesus Christ? That doesn't even make sense.

I was with friends now and needed to respect their beliefs, so I did as they asked and kept quiet as we passed the protestors. I did tell Andrew and Audrey, "I believe that the LDS Church is the most misunderstood religion in the world. I've been misunderstood my whole life!"

At the Hill Cumorah Pageant, hundreds of cast members in costume mingled with the audience before the performance began. We approached a group of them in long Native American–looking robes. I asked if we could get a picture with "you ladies," and they all turned to us.

"Well, yes, but I'm a man." We all cracked up laughing. Holy cow, typical me!

The Hill Cumorah Pageant was bigger than any Broadway musical I've ever attended. It was filled with pyrotechnics and water shooting in all directions. It depicts scenes from the Book of Mormon with water blasting all over to represent a storm, fire blazing as a wicked king persecutes the people of God, and angels coming from the sky down onto the stage.

Standing with the "ladies" from the cast of the Hill Cumorah Pageant

Darin had constantly been with me for two days now, and he was not ready to leave my side yet. Throughout the performance, my eyes welled up with tears as my unexplained feelings continued to overflow. It was still so bizarre that I was crying so much, but my body had to release the emotional buildup somehow.

Throughout the two days, with the exception of going to Niagara Falls, Andrew noticed I carried that "stolen" copy of the Book of Mormon everywhere. It was always on my person, every minute. I didn't even realize I was doing it, but it was the anchor to keep me steady through these huge waves of emotion. I needed it in my hand.

Another thing Andrew noticed—which I had no idea about until more than a year later—was that day, my phrasing changed in how I related myself to the Church. I had started the trip by asking about things that *the Church* does or believes. By the time we were on our way to the Hill Cumorah Pageant, I was asking what *WE* do or believe. Without even realizing it, I had begun including myself in the Church's membership and family.

That night at the hotel, we checked LDS Finder to discover a Church building and service time in my zip code. Bingo. There's a ward thirteen minutes from my home address. I still didn't quite believe that I could attend Sunday services in an actual Church building, but they reassured me that attendance restrictions are only for the temple. Sundays are for everyone. We talked about how life-changing this trip was and looked at some of our photos. Andrew is a photographer, and we airdropped more than seven hundred pictures from those forty-eight hours. I have come to appreciate all of those photos as a reminder of my journey into this new venture in life.

Before I headed back to Connecticut the next day, I stopped at the Sacred Grove again. I found Sister Guimaras for a third time at the visitors' center. Because of the pageant, the foyer was packed full of people, but she focused on me and asked if we could pray together as if we were the only ones there. She grabbed my hands, and the floodgates opened yet again. My crying quickly turned to sobbing and gasping. I felt like people were staring at us, but I didn't care. There was so much in my mind, but one single thought took over my brain: *I think I'm actually going to become Mormon! I want to get baptized!*

I went back out to the Sacred Grove alone to read and ponder some verses in the Book of Mormon that Andrew and Audrey had marked for me. They had also each written a note in the front cover of my book before they left for the airport.

> We don't always understand the challenges we face in life and it can be difficult, but through Christ we can be healed if we have faith in and rely on Him. But it's not only about faith, it's about action. I believe you have felt the influence of the Holy Ghost powerfully this weekend and hope you never forget those feelings. . . . We don't always need to know everything, especially at first, but it starts with a desire to know or a hope. Every page of this book testifies how much you are loved by God. I know this and now it's your turn to learn for yourself.

Palmyra, the Hill Cumorah, and the Sacred Grove are truly sacred ground. I did not expect to be so open to receiving revelation, but I had felt Darin's presence the entire time and knew he wanted me to do this for both of us. I am in shock at how much just two days can change someone's life forever.

On my drive home, I turned on my iTunes and started a playlist as usual. It was the same list I had wanted to hear when I was driving out to Pennsylvania. A song by Madonna came on and oh my goodness, I had never in my life noticed how many times she uses the Lord's name in vain. She's always been risqué, but this was crossing so many lines. After spending just two days with these friends from Utah, I was starting to hear and say things like oh my goodness, darn, and holy stars! I wasn't ready to accept all of the changes that were coming, but here was a change I totally didn't expect. I just couldn't listen to "B**** I'm Madonna." First my vocabulary and now even my taste in music was changing immediately! It was a definite indication that this religion thing was going somewhere.

When I got back to Connecticut, I drove straight to a beautiful location that I frequent often to pray and reflect while staring into the Connecticut River. Nature has always been a place where I can feel God's presence. I spent at least an hour reading the scriptures and looking up at the sky as if to commune with Darin and have a study session with him. As I read, I could feel the tension of life release each time I exhaled.

I made a video to text to Andrew and Audrey.

"I'm standing at the Connecticut River. I just got home, watching the sunset. I just wanted to do a video testimonial thanking you for what an amazing, life-changing experience it was being with you guys. I think of you as family and I always will. I love you both very much, and I just want to say from the bottom of my heart, thank you for saving my life."

Chapter 7

Meet the Mormons

Think of how you felt when for the first time you believed
and understood that you are truly a child of God.[5]

~ Dieter F. Uchtdorf

There were four days between when I returned to Connecticut and when I would attend church for the first time. That's a lot of time for doubt, frustration, confusion, and just plain fear to set in. I also felt a lot of pressure of obligation. I had told multiple people that I would attend the local ward that Sunday. They were expecting it—how could I *not* go? If I didn't follow through, what would I say when they started texting to ask me about it?

On Saturday evening, I drove to the church to check things out while no one was there. My palms were sweating. I might have even had a couple of tears in my eyes because I was so high-strung. I grabbed the Book of Mormon that I had taken from the hotel in Utah and walked around the church. That security blanket again. I thought it would relax me if I counted the parking spaces. Who does that? There are 289.

When I got home, I decided to iron my white dress shirt for church the next day. I've been ironing my clothes all my life, but I've never had one just randomly burst into flames. Which happened right then. I yanked out the cord on the iron and grabbed a glass of water to dump on my burning shirt and ironing board. *How does this happen?*

I had at least a dozen other white shirts, but of course every single one either had a ring on the collar or was too tight. I raced out to Marshalls to buy a new shirt and made it just in time before they closed. I wasn't able to buy a new iron and ironing board and ended up borrowing a neighbor's.

Sunday, July 23, 2017. Time for church. It was a gloriously sunny morning with no clouds or wind. I was only one block away from the church when suddenly the huge limb of a tree fell from the sky onto the passenger side of my car. It hit my front bumper and made its way up the hood, scraping along the side all the way to the back of the trunk. *God, are you joking? Who has a tree fall on their car in perfect weather? Is this a comedy show?*

I couldn't even stop to assess the damage. I just kept driving. I started to get this funny laugh, knowing that if I stopped to look at the damage, it would sidetrack me and I wouldn't enter the Church building.

Oh my heavens! I nervously parked my car, reached for my security Book of Mormon, and slowly made my way to the front door. I could feel others looking at me and I was shaking so badly I'm surprised I didn't drop anything. I was approached by a woman in the entrance lobby.

"Hi, are you visiting from out of town?" Her tone was very cheerful and friendly.

"No, I'm a walk-in."

She paused. "Come again?"

"Yes, I'm a walk-in. I've never been here before."

Her eyes widened. "Oh, um, well, okay, my heavens. Let me find our sister missionaries. I'll be right back—don't go anywhere." She rushed away into the chapel.

My thoughts were rapid fire. *Dennis, she just said don't go anywhere. You could still run. Run! She obviously didn't know how to answer. I guess it's really unusual have a walk-in. Why aren't you running?!*

Earlier that week, Shelby had tried to call the bishop to inform him that I would be coming as an investigator. But the number listed on LDS.org was a pizza parlor. Every phone number they tried was disconnected or incorrect. So no one at the ward knew I was coming.

The sister missionaries burst out the double doors and introduced themselves as Sister Esplin and Sister Tumlinson. They were maybe a little too peachy or exuberant but filled with a lively spirit.

During sacrament meeting, the two sisters sat me down between them as if they could sense my urge to bolt and wanted to prevent that. They both held hymnals during the songs, angled so I could see the words because I'd never heard these songs before. *Do I look to my right or to my left?* They sang loudly and smiled encouragingly as I tried to join in. My mind was jumping around during the entire service. I wondered about possible damage to my car. I felt like everyone was staring at me because they knew I was an outsider who was not a member of the Church.

They prayed really weird—everyone crossed their arms like they were angry, and bowed their heads and didn't look up at anything. How rude! Definitely not the prayers I was accustomed to seeing while attending other Christian denominations. Once it was explained, however, it makes total sense. This is how Mormons teach children proper reverence and respect for God during prayer—to be still and quiet so you're not distracted by what's around you or misbehaving to interrupt others. It's a helpful way to meditate, focus, and be centered on the Holy Ghost. But it was quite startling the first time I observed it.

During the sacrament, or communion, I leaned to a sister and asked if I was allowed to partake. Oh yes! This was another new thing—I'd never been to a church that allowed nonmembers to participate in the rite of the Lord's Supper. I also wondered about the offering basket because this is a big thing in every church I had ever attended. But Mormons make their financial contributions privately. No one knows the amount anyone gives except the person charged with actually counting the money and making the bank deposit, and it's kept strictly confidential.

After the meeting, I stood with the sisters at the back of the chapel, feeling like I'd crashed a family reunion and was being welcomed like the long-lost cousin. I was greeted nonstop by everyone who walked past us. LOTS of introductions. It seemed like I met the entire ward in less than ten minutes. I was overwhelmed. But loved. LOVED. The same as with Shelby and Sister Guimaras. A friend told me later that in her entire life in the Church, she's always seen visitors welcomed by friendly members. But she'd never seen anyone so thoroughly pounced on to be welcomed into a ward.

Church was nowhere near being over. *Three hours? What on earth could they achieve in three hours, and who attends that long? Only the Mormons, I guess.*

The second class was called Gospel Principles. I was asked to introduce myself and share my story of why I had decided to randomly show up at their ward that day. I talked about what happened on my way to the Priesthood Restoration Site and my time in Palmyra. I talked a lot about Darin. Everyone seemed far more surprised and excited about my experiences in Palmyra than they were about the idea that I'd received spiritual guidance from my deceased brother. That didn't get much of a reaction—it seemed to be rather normal to them.

For the third hour, the men and women separate into different classes, so the sisters left me! I'd been with them for the past two hours, so where were they going? Who was going to answer my questions? Well, I didn't need to worry about that. Two of the men sat on either side of me, and one of them was whispering in my ear most of the time. I couldn't tell you what the instructor said about anything, but by the end of the class, I had the wireless password to the church and every single LDS app downloaded onto my phone. Holy cow, how many apps could one church have? I now had the LDS library with all of the scriptures and lesson manuals, LDS tools, meetinghouse locator, Family Search, Ancestry, and even an app that allows me to order the elders to come to my house for blessings. I shouldn't bother with paying for the family history sites because they would be free as soon as I was baptized and got a membership number.

Free? Where's the money coming from? Does everyone here work as professional network marketers making residual income? What the heck is an LDS number? Does that replace my social security card? More and more questions swirled around in my head. Yes, Mormons really do have ID numbers, and I thought that sounded pretty cool. They have all the other denominations beat on that one.

After church, the sister missionaries came to find me quickly and asked when we could meet during the week for some lessons. I thought about signing them up on my team because they would make great network marketers, but I had made a vow to myself to never mix church and state. No crossing work into my church life.

I said I'd call them the next day to set something up, and they handed me a whole mass of brochures with their names and phone number written everywhere! I asked if we could get a picture together so I could text it to my friends in Utah so they would know that I actually went to church. I'm sure they were wondering if I'd go through with my commitment to attend that day. I wish I could have seen the look on their faces when they got a photo of me with two sister missionaries holding the Book of Mormon.

When I called the sisters the next day, we had a cheerful conversation, and I said I'd like to take them to lunch. "I'm really looking forward to getting to know you better. I have some private information to share and a lot of questions. Is there anything you need me to bring?"

They said I should bring a copy of the Bible, and we got off the phone. That confused me. *I thought the Book of Mormon was the new Bible.* But sure, whatever. The lightbulb came on later that the Book of Mormon's subtitle is "Another Testament of Jesus Christ." It goes *with* the Bible; it does not replace it. The Church of Jesus Christ uses both.

I learned later that this phone call was on speakerphone while the sisters were in a car with two elders, on their way to Boston for a

First day at church with Sister Esplin and Sister Tumlinson

meeting with their mission president. The elders were extremely leery of me and concerned for the sisters' safety. "Don't trust this guy. He's a fake. Nobody could be so eager to meet with missionaries. You definitely should bring someone from the ward with you. He said he was supposed to be a referral from Utah but you never received a call and the bishop never received a call. He's probably some crazy off the street looking to take advantage of young women. Don't see him alone!" I do relate to Elder Little's need to protect his fellow missionaries—I've become very protective of the sisters as well.

I had recently moved, so my life was in boxes. I own several Bibles and have a beautiful leather-bound Bible that was given to me by a dear friend for my confirmation in the Congregational church. I couldn't find any of them that day, so I asked my mother if I could borrow one of the many Bibles she has at her house. She didn't think anything of it and said, "Of course."

When I arrived at her house to pick it up, she asked why I wanted it, and I told her I was meeting with the Mormon missionaries. She very quickly snatched it out of my hands. "I'm not allowing you to bring that Bible to meet with those Mormons." I was shocked. For years, my parents have been rather forcefully trying to get me to go to church and study the Bible. Now that I'm actually doing it and asking to read the Bible, she does this? How could someone who claims to be Christian refuse her own son one of multiple Bibles that are lying around her house? I had never told them that I had been church hopping for years—I had kept that private because it was a personal search I needed to do. My parents knew that I'd gone to Latter-day Saint historical sites in New York, but I doubt that it ever crossed their minds that their outspoken gay advocate son would actually consider *becoming* a Mormon.

My father was equally as horrified that I had the Book of Mormon and was going to study with missionaries. "What is this? Are you doing this to advance your business, because your company is based in Utah?"

I cautiously shared that I was considering being baptized, and I heard the same lecture I've heard for most of my life. "We love you, but we don't accept or approve of your chosen lifestyle." I was so frustrated. First of all, this thing about a "chosen" lifestyle was way past its prime—who would actually *choose* to be gay? Did my parents *choose* to be straight?

At least they had the "choice" part right about studying with the missionaries and reading the Book of Mormon. I did feel spiritually compelled to move forward with it, and I felt like Darin was highly encouraging it from the Other Side. But it was still my decision.

My parents' antagonism did not deter me. In fact, it had the opposite effect—it caused me to go even deeper into my study of the Book of Mormon and the Church. I started reading and studying as much as I could take in. Every time I read, I felt joy and spiritual strength and I knew that I was on the path God wanted for me.

Chapter 8

Two Steps Forward, One Step Back

> I know that he loveth his children; nevertheless,
> I do not know the meaning of all things.
>
> ~ 1 Nephi 11:17

My beautiful sister missionaries gave up eighteen months of their lives to serve Heavenly Father, and one of their commissions was to teach me about the gospel of Christ and The Church of Jesus Christ of Latter-day Saints.

Two days after attending a Latter-day Saint ward for the first time, I met them at a Panera café and told them to order whatever they wanted. My palms were sweaty, and I started rambling with a lot of nervous chatter. I was probably bragging about my company's owners in Utah, telling them for the eleventh time that the founders of my company are Mormon. I'm sure I said something stupid like, "I just love my Mormon friends!"

When we sat down with our food, I was still babbling and then abruptly announced, "I'm gay! Please share with me your views on homosexuality. Do you have any gay friends in the LDS Church?"

I wondered if I threw these poor teenagers for a loop, but they handled it well. One told me that she has a good friend who is gay. The other shared a story about her mother briefly meeting one of the General Authorities and whispered to him that she has a family member who is gay. His reply was, "Everything will all work out." The sisters' responses aren't depicted well in writing—when you read it, it's just words. But if you'd been there, when we were together having this conversation, those words would carry much more weight and assurance. It was as if a higher power was speaking through them rather than them just telling me things on their own. They felt my sorrow and pain as they took it on as their own. I had a comforting and warm sense of security.

I apologized for not bringing a copy of the Bible and told them about trying to borrow one from my mother. This didn't bother them. They cheerfully said with big smiles, "Would you like to have a copy of the Bible?" Sister Esplin reached into a bag and pulled out a Bible and handed it to me. "You can keep it!"

What the heck is going on here? They give out free Bibles too! I've already stolen a Book of Mormon that I could have gotten for free from the missionaries, and now a Bible too? I couldn't have been happier.

Unfortunately, I was also thinking that I would take it to my mother and rub it in her face. *You wouldn't loan me one of your Bibles, so the sisters just gave me one. Isn't that lovely, Mom?* When she would tell me it wasn't the real Bible, I would say, *Oh, I don't know, why don't you look and see if it has the Old and New Testaments?* Yes, this is something I need to work on. I soon learned from Sister Tumlinson and Sister Esplin that a core of the Latter-day Saint religion is to choose to be like Christ—to listen to others, lead by example, and be good to all. We are NOT to participate in drama and create conflict with others. It's not about me; it's about how I can help you, no matter what your faith and beliefs are.

The official message that day was a lesson about the plan of salvation, which I had already heard from Andrew and Audrey. This time, the sisters created a little diagram as a dot-to-dot puzzle, and when the lines were drawn in, I saw immediately that it spelled out the word *love.* Part of me still had a hard time fully grasping what Shelby had been telling me for months about God's love, so I asked these sisters, "Am I going to hell for being gay? Does God really hate me for being gay?" They assured me, like Shelby and Sister Guimaras and Andrew and Audrey had, that God loves me very much. I spent most of the lesson with tears in my eyes.

At the end of the lesson, they asked, "Will you commit to living your life according to the plan of salvation?" Yes, yes, and yes! I was so excited to be part of this wonderful church where the people are so loving!

They also asked me if I would be baptized, which right then, I wanted very badly. But I asked, "That won't be for a long time, right?" They said it would be whenever I was ready, whether that was months or weeks. I almost fully burst into tears as I exclaimed, "I thought I would have to wait years for this!"

We set a time for the next lesson later in the week, and I asked a complete stranger to take a picture of the three of us. I was doing it to send to friends in Utah to verify that I was meeting with the missionaries. I was delighted to learn later that members are encouraged to journal and record their personal histories as they happen, so in difficult times, they can reflect on the happy and spiritual moments of their lives. I was starting it then without even realizing.

I posted the picture on Facebook with the caption: "Guess who I happened to run into at Panera? These two lovely sister missionaries are serving our Heavenly Father. So I decided to buy them lunch #spreadlove." I knew that people in my Utah company would understand what was happening, but really, it was a bit of a white lie. I kept it vague for people who already knew I was friendly and would talk to anyone, and they didn't need to suspect anything else.

Over the next few days, my Book of Mormon became quite colorful with highlighters and

First lesson with the sister missionaries

sticky arrows to color code the lessons and things I found interesting. I loved how the scriptures focused on the teaching of Christ to love one another. The people in the Book of Mormon were taught to be kind to each other, with a heavy emphasis on service. As I dove deeper into my study, I found many similarities to the Holy Bible. It took me back to when I was studying for my confirmation in the Congregational church. As "Another Testament of Jesus Christ," the Book of Mormon had further answers to my personal questions that the Bible hadn't been able to answer and that were brushed off during my Confirmation classes as a teenager. For example, I've always wondered why various churches only sprinkle water for baptisms when Jesus was baptized in the Jordan River. The Church of Jesus Christ practices full immersion, as the Savior did.

For my next lesson, we met at the home of some members of the ward. Kit and Stephen were just as I pictured the people in the Book of Mormon—extremely warm and friendly. I remember sitting in their beautiful, all-white living room, but I don't remember much of what was said because I was nervous and overwhelmed and excited. I probably rambled a lot again. The second lesson was about the Restoration of the gospel and the organization of the Church, which Andrew and Audrey had first talked to me about in the Sacred Grove. The Restoration *happened* in the Sacred Grove! And I'd been there! I remembered some of it but was glad for the repetition so I could learn it better. The sisters asked me again at the end of this lesson, "Will you commit to following the restored gospel of Jesus Christ?" Yes, yes, and yes! If I could have captured their smiles . . . they had such joy!

My second time at church, we took more pictures. This is how I've ended up journaling everything—through photos. The countless photos have allowed me to remember much more than if I'd just written things down or recorded nothing at all. As I shot pictures with the sisters, I asked for their parents' cell phone numbers. The sisters were allowed to talk to their families only on specific holidays during their mission, but I could text them whenever I want. You can't believe how elated their parents were—they loved receiving the updates I sent frequently.

I was surprised when I was invited back to Kit's home without the sisters doing a lesson at the same time. She asked me to have dinner with her family and another couple from the ward. It was a taste of heaven, literally as well as figuratively. Kit is from Hong Kong, and I told her about the time I had spent in Asia years ago. She prepared an authentic Asian feast, which was amazing. I wasn't nervous because how can you be nervous with all that delicious food in front of you?

The fellowship was also remarkable. I enjoyed it so much that I hated for the evening to end.

I texted Andrew to tell him how things were going, and this was his reply: "Audrey and I were just commenting to each other that we can see a very positive change about you from a couple weeks ago to now. Remember that we said we can sometimes tell when someone is a member of the Church. We see a difference! Keep it up!"

Lesson three was at the community center along the majestic Connecticut River. I thought it would be nice to do our lesson while walking down the viewing path. It was another gorgeous day, but suddenly my iPhone started blaring with an emergency service warning. It said to seek shelter because there were tornados in the area—what on earth?! It was beautiful outside!

When the sisters arrived, they caught me off guard by saying that someone from the ward would be joining us as well. I thought it would be nice to get to know him but wondered why he was there in the first place. We went inside the community center because my iPhone was still going off with multiple weather alerts, and as soon as I started the opening prayer, we heard a series of loud crashes and bangs from thunder and lightning. As I said *Amen*, the lights went out. There turned out to be power outages all over the state with major wind and hail warnings and massive flash flooding. If we'd still been walking out by the river, I could have gotten the sisters swept away!

The center had backup generators, so when the lights came back on, we went ahead with the lesson, which was beautiful: faith, repentance, baptism, the gift of the Holy Ghost, and enduring to the end. We focused on the Holy Ghost and the comfort He brings, and I understood that I had already felt the Holy Ghost multiple times confirming that I was making the necessary changes for my life. Enduring was already a concept I was very familiar with, so that took no effort to accept.

"Will you commit to follow the gospel of Jesus Christ?" Yes, yes, and yes!

Then the sisters threw me for a loop. "We've been fasting and praying about a baptismal date for you, and we came up with two dates."

I froze. "I'm sorry, what?"

"August 12 or August 19." Sister Tumlinson looked straight at me very expectantly. She had no hesitation at all about this scheduling.

I opened my mouth but nothing came out at first. I stammered, "Um, isn't that a little fast?" I of course wanted to be baptized, but I didn't think it would be *that* soon! Wasn't there more to learn first?

"Those are the dates that came to us."

I whipped out my phone and opened the calendar. August 12 wouldn't work because I had a work conference that day. So it would have to be the 19th, and I was ecstatic. As soon as I gave my answer out loud, I thought, *Wait, what? What did I just commit to? Maybe I should see a therapist. Am I having a mid-life crisis? I am about the right age for a mid-life crisis.*

The sisters went happily on their way, but the man who had joined our lesson had more to say to me. He told me that he had shared my story with his sister in Utah who is a therapist. She apparently had worked with dozens of "straight LDS people dealing with same-sex attraction" with a 100 percent success ratio but had never had the opportunity of working with an authentically gay man. He hoped I would be interested in speaking with her.

Authentic gay man? I've been called a lot of things but I've never been referred to as an "authentic gay man." That sounds like the *Mona Lisa* painting that belongs in a museum.

He appeared entirely oblivious that my face turned bright red, and I felt like I'd been punched in the stomach. I was speechless, and all I wanted to do was run. I had committed to joining the Church because I thought I would be accepted as I am and no one would try to make me straight. And here was this person telling me about conversion therapy with someone in Utah who works with straight people with same-sex attraction? "Straight people with same-sex attraction" doesn't even make sense!

Every question and doubt came crashing down like the thunder and lightning storm we'd just sat through, and this guy just kept talking. I finally made the excuse that I had another appointment, so he gave me his sister's contact information and said she was expecting my call. I was even more horrified and abashed that he expected me to talk to her and almost ran to my car. I may have burned rubber off my tires as I peeled out of the parking lot.

Without remembering how I got there, I found myself at a quiet spot along the river, a *different* spot than at the community center. I was shattered—what on earth had just happened? I sat there crying.

When was a church family going to accept me as I am? Out of the blue, my phone rang and it was the sisters. They were calling to remind me about a Book of Mormon study class that evening at the church. I sobbed out that I wasn't going to go, and I could hear the shock in their voices: "*What's wrong?*"

I stumbled through an explanation of what had just happened, and they were very quick to say that it would be taken care of as soon as possible. They asked me to please attend the Book of Mormon study group as planned, and we would talk more about this situation then. And they abruptly hung up.

I sat there clutching my scriptures and remembered something Andrew had warned me about while we were in New York. "You're going to find some—not all, but a few—Mormons who may not follow the gospel to a T, just like in any religion. There are some good Mormons, and there are some not-so-good Mormons." Now I saw that there are also uninformed Mormons—people who mean well but who have never been around gay people, so they don't know or understand our social and cultural situation and have no comprehension of the trauma of conversion therapy. I've never suspected this man of being malicious or wanting to offend me; in fact, I believe he would be horrified to learn that he did.

As I thought through all of this, what came into my mind was from God: "Be more like Christ. Listen to others. Let's turn up the love, lead by example, and most important, just be yourself." People would soon realize that I'm just like them, a normal human being—who happens to be gay.

I did attend the study group that evening. The sisters had called their mission leader in Boston, and he was going to come down to Hartford to meet me and conduct my baptismal interview that Sunday. They also wanted to introduce me to Knox, an LGBT convert in the Boston area who had fully committed to being a member of The Church of Jesus Christ of Latter-day Saints. Someone like me! Hooray!

I called Shelby and texted Andrew soon after. "The sister missionaries have me on a fast-forward track to baptism. It feels rushed, but at the same time, it feels right. I have a sense of peace and calm."

My next lesson was at another member's home. Paula was one of the first people I met at the ward and has been a wonderful friend ever since. She made blueberry cobbler for us, just for the occasion. The sisters and I talked about the Word of Wisdom, the Church's health code. I already knew the rule about no tea, coffee, alcohol, smoking, or illegal drugs. I had never used any of these substances with frequency anyway, so it was not a chore to give them up. We mainly discussed the benefits of good health and living by the guidelines in the Word of Wisdom.

I had an *aha!* moment when talking about maintaining good gut health. This is something I've been teaching through my business, and now I saw where the company owners got it from—the Word of Wisdom.

August 6 was my first fast Sunday. I had no idea what that was— that we give up two meals and water to show God our intention to focus while we pray, ponder, and reflect on answers we receive from the Holy Ghost. As I sat with the sisters in sacrament meeting, I apologized for not fasting. They were quick to reassure me. "Oh, no worries, it's our fault because we forgot to tell you."

I was very interested to see that on the first Sunday of every month, people just get up to share their feelings and testify of God and Christ. There's no planned speaker. I don't know what caused me to do this (well, I do now—the Holy Ghost. And Darin.), but I leaned over to Sister Esplin and asked, "Am I allowed to go up there?" She looked surprised but said that I could.

So I went up to the podium, not having any idea what I would say. And now, I don't even remember what I ended up saying at all. But I do remember feeling the strong presence of Heavenly Father and the Holy Ghost.

When I sat back down, both sisters whispered to me, "That was incredible!" Sister Esplin whispered in my ear, "When my mission is over, you are going to be the first man I hug." Once missionaries are set apart to serve our Heavenly Father, they're not allowed to hug members of the opposite sex.

After the service, many ward members thanked me for sharing my thoughts and feelings and said how moved they were by it. If only I knew what I said! Sister Esplin's journal later clued me in. Her entry from that day said:

When it was time for people to bear their testimonies, Dennis leaned over and asked if he was allowed to go up. I said of course! So he got right up and bore such a powerful testimony. He declared that he knew this is the true church. The chapel is usually loud with children, but it was silent as Dennis was speaking. When he came back, he leaned over and told me that it wasn't him speaking. He is a public speaker for his occupation and he knows it wasn't him. I told him it was the Holy Ghost and he got teary-eyed. It's so fun to see him on his journey!

Oh, wow! Really?

On that same day, I received a text in the middle of church from my father saying that he and my mother had decided to attend my baptismal service. I had already told them that I intended to be baptized into The Church of Jesus Christ of Latter-day Saints, and they were adamantly opposed. "It's a cult," they said. "It's of the devil." They originally refused to attend my baptism. Then they did want to attend. Then they didn't. Now they were back to saying they'd decided to go. The back-and-forth was aggravating.

I shared the text with the sisters, and the thought came to me that this was the perfect time for my parents to meet them. Even though I'd invited them, I decided that I would only agree to their attendance if they met beforehand with the sisters to learn about Latter-day Saint beliefs.

The sisters rearranged their schedule to meet with my parents that afternoon and decided to discuss with them the Articles of Faith, a series of statements that Joseph Smith made about our basic beliefs. We believe in Jesus Christ, we believe in baptism, we believe in seeking after good things, etc. I was so grateful for their calm composure even though Sister Esplin admitted to being very nervous about meeting them. But we all prayed that my parents' hearts would be softened and that the visit would have no animosity between all the participants.

The discussion went much more smoothly than anyone thought it would. The first thing my father asked was whether I would be allowed to receive blood transfusions, surgery, or other medical procedures. (Wrong religion, Dad.) My mother wouldn't really look the sisters in the eye, and that was very awkward, but she eventually warmed up to them. She even gave them a hug when we all said goodbye at the end.

I do appreciate my parents' willingness to meet with the sisters and listen to even the basics of a church they disagree with. I love them very much. One of my own challenges is learning to forgive, and this was a perfect opportunity to put into practice the things I'd been learning about Christlike behavior. Heavenly Father wants me to love my parents and get along well with them, forgive them for the past, and move on into the future with an open heart.

The time spent with my parents and the sisters helped me feel more comfortable with the "two steps forward, one step back" internal dance I was doing as I engaged more and more with the Church of Jesus Christ.

The next week, I met Knox from Boston in person. We had already connected on social media and spoken on the phone. It was like talking to my twin. He attended my next meeting with the sisters (number six!) and we talked about the Ten Commandments. Knox had attained a college degree in religious studies and is a scriptorian. He didn't carry any of the scriptures, but he could quote verses from the Bible and Book of Mormon verbatim without looking anything up, like a walking library. I aspire to that kind of learning.

In the lesson, he compared the Israelite exodus out of Egypt to the LGBT community. "The Ten Commandments form a key part of a larger, literal coming-out narrative in Exodus. When the Israelites were enslaved in Egypt, they couldn't be themselves and had no independent identity. When the Lord led them out of Egypt, He gave them a covenant that formed the core part of their new identity. They now were to live fully as themselves, with commandments to ensure the presence of justice and tranquility. I think this narrative is liberative for LGBTQ folks who want to know about a God who leads people from confinement to a place where they can be themselves."

As we left the discussion, we realized that the sisters had locked their keys in the trunk of their car. I was happy to call the locksmith Darin had worked for many years ago, and they quickly came even though it was after hours. What a blessing—I took it as another sign that Darin was working for my conversion to the Church from the next life.

My brother was often the focus of my lessons with the sister missionaries, particularly when we talked about the plan of salvation and temple work in behalf of the deceased. I had told the sisters everything that had happened in upstate New York, including hearing "I Can Only Imagine" when I asked for a sign from God and feeling Darin's presence throughout my visit to Palmyra. So I was especially interested when they told me about proxy baptisms for the dead.

The temple had been considered foreign, off limits, weird. I'd previously never had a desire to go, even when I could have. When the Hartford Connecticut Temple completed construction in 2016, I was asked multiple times by friends in Utah if I would attend the public open house. I drove past it all the time, but I had no interest and thought, *Why on earth would I do that?* Shelby continually reassured me that the Latter-day Saint members would accept me as a gay man, but there was something in me at that time that didn't quite believe her. So no, I didn't want to go to the temple open house.

Now with lessons, talks with the sisters, and my own research on LDS.org, I had a strong desire to do Darin's baptism for him in a temple. I felt that Darin himself was insistent that I do it, and that was part of why he'd been the catalyst with my revelation in New York. I wondered if I would still feel his spiritual presence and communicate with him after I completed his ordinance, or if that would fade away as he moved on to other things. I had no answers, but I was developing faith.

I met with the sisters two more times that week. At a Book of Mormon study night, I volunteered to offer the group prayer, and in it I said, "Thank you for placing these two sisters in my life. I have a feeling we will be friends for a long time." Sister Esplin was so sweet when she said that she never wants to lose contact with me. The feeling is definitely mutual.

My birthday was that Friday, and we had a lesson at the park. There was no cake and there were no presents, but the gift of gospel learning is more valuable than any object that can be placed in a box with a bow.

When I'm with members of the Church, and especially when I'm with missionaries, I can feel the Holy Ghost. The sisters were so full of faith and love that whenever I was with them, I couldn't help but follow along, and I knew whatever they asked of me was the right thing. I could jump in head first with no hesitation or fear.

The challenge was when I was alone. When the sisters left, their faith and strength went with them, and then everything seemed to be going much too fast. I was hesitant and uncertain. I didn't have the gift of the Holy Ghost yet—the constant companionship—so when I was alone, the adversary started kicking and screaming. Doubt and fear would completely take over and churn up tremendous emotional turmoil. I'm not bipolar, but it sure felt like that sometimes.

There are questions I still don't have answers to. What's going to happen if (when?) I find myself interested in pursuing a romantic relationship with a man again? What happens when the desire to have a life-long companion resurfaces? It's not like there's a refund system or thirty-day money-back guarantee when you make a commitment to God.

I had to learn to just give it to God, no matter what my church membership status was. I also regularly called on my brother for help and support in those dark moments. Darin, even from the next life, has never let me down.

Unfortunately, I had no plans for my birthday beyond meeting with the sisters, and that evening, the mental swinging was in full force. *What are you doing? Today is your birthday and you're home alone when you should be out celebrating.* The spiral down was so fast that I couldn't even think to reach for the scriptures or pick up the phone and call someone.

Forward. I remembered that in exactly a week, I would be picking up Derek and Shelby at the airport when they flew in to perform my baptism. The pressure of expectation from them and everyone else in Utah knowing about my joining the Church kept the lid on my emotional turmoil.

Backward. *Wouldn't it be nice to go out and find someone to spend the evening with, to feel the connection of personal touch with another man? Just one more time!*

Forward. *I'm worth more than a one-night stand. I have strong morals, and I'm better than that.* Knowing the support I had from Utah helped to lessen the fear and hesitation the adversary was planting in my mind, and I was able to pull through that night without compromising myself. I know a lot of people were praying for me that week.

The next day was my work conference near Hartford, but I woke up in excruciating pain. I'd been having internal issues with my bladder and urinary tract off and on all summer, including pain that threatened to prevent me from going to New York with Andrew and Audrey. But this was worse. I didn't want to go to the hospital because I had people flying in to Hartford for our conference, and I was one of the hosts. Plus, I was supposed to have my interview with the mission president the next day. I knew my doctor would not just call in an antibiotic, as she had done once previously. So I pushed through the pain and kept getting ready for my work conference.

When I arrived there, I was almost unable to walk because I was in so much pain. It was pretty obvious that something was very wrong, and one of my colleagues immediately pulled me aside. She is a doctor, so I told her what was happening, and she insisted that I leave immediately for the hospital. If I didn't, I would soon be taken there by ambulance anyway.

I called the sister missionaries while I was driving to the hospital. They asked for the hospital's address, and said they would call the elders to come with them to administer an oil blessing to help the sick and afflicted. Sure, what did I have to lose? I had no idea what I was in for.

I arrived at the hospital, parked my car like a drunk person, and practically crawled into the emergency department. A nurse immediately grabbed a wheelchair, and I was taken right away to a private room. I told them that the missionaries were coming—two boys with white shirts and ties—and to let them come to my room as soon as they arrived.

A doctor came in and did an ultrasound on my abdomen. She then immediately ordered a catheter to clear my system. I pretty much freaked out. I didn't want anyone sticking a catheter in me! She said very sternly that I needed to calm down. They were starting an IV to get me some pain medication, and then they would proceed.

Two nurses administered morphine through the IV, and I felt a numbing and tingling sensation go through my entire body from head to toe. Shortly after, they started to insert the catheter, and I screamed bloody murder. I felt as if I was going to pass out. They wanted me to just breathe and calm down, but the pain was too agonizing. More morphine and a sedative, but that wasn't working. Once they were done with the catheter, I was still shouting. I overheard doctors nearby: "Do something to calm him down! He's scaring other patients!"

Another doctor interjected, "Get those little boys back here! They might be able to calm him down!" Apparently, the elders had arrived and were sitting in the waiting room.

When the two elders walked in, I was still in so much pain that I wanted to burst out screaming, and my body was being flushed out with bags of saline. But interestingly, as soon as I saw them, I was able to breathe deeply through the pain and even talk to them and the nurse.

The attending nurse had the personality of a piranha and was not happy that the elders showed up. She treated us all respectfully, but there was definitely some tension. We figured out quickly that she actually lived in the same apartment building as the elders, and they had carried her groceries from her car to her door just a few days previously. I thought that was the coolest thing!

"Oh wow! That's amazing! The missionaries give up two years of their lives to serve our Heavenly Father, so I love to send photos to their parents. Would you mind if I took a photo of the three of you to send to their parents?" I was surprised when she agreed to do it, and then she stepped out.

In the Church, elders are ordained to the Melchizedek Priesthood, which bestows on them the keys and ability to offer blessings with consecrated oil to heal the sick. Since we were alone, the elders asked if they could perform a blessing, and I eagerly said yes. I was still in a tremendous amount of pain despite a crazy amount of painkillers, and I would have accepted pretty much anything for it to ease. They asked who I wanted to pronounce the blessing, and I said whoever was newest so he could have some practice. The first part of the blessing is done with exact phrasing, and poor Elder Christensen was so nervous that he messed up and had to start over. I said, "It's okay, just relax. It's not like you're going to kill me!"

A little drop of oil was poured onto my head, and the elders spoke through the Holy Ghost, offering comfort and relief and stating that the doctors would be guided to find the best treatment possible. As I was lying there, I had a sense of extreme calmness, no pain, and I felt like I was floating. With my eyes closed, I saw what appeared to be a gray light through a tunnel. I began to pray fervently on behalf of the elders: *Oh, please don't take me now, God. If they finish this blessing and*

I flatline in front of them, these poor elders will never be the same. They'll probably fly back home to Utah tomorrow.

When they closed the prayer, I still felt like I was floating. It was just like every movie I've ever seen or book I've ever read about near-death experiences. But when I opened my eyes and looked at the two elders, I didn't feel like I should share what had just happened. I didn't want to scare them.

Sister Esplin and Sister Tumlinson came in right after the blessing, and the five of us talked for a while. The doctor came in and said that I needed to be admitted to the hospital and receive a blood transfusion. I know the chances of contracting HIV are next to none, but I'm still very afraid of diseases. I asked all four missionaries if they would be willing to be tested to see if we matched blood types. All said they definitely would do it. That brought me a lot of comfort. Not to sound like I'm discriminating, but I did feel like they had clean blood.

The doctor left and the piranha nurse came back to change the IV bag. While she was doing that, she avoided eye contact but told us that she was very uncomfortable with the photo I had taken earlier and wanted me to delete it immediately. She even insisted on watching me delete it off my phone. After she left, I looked at the elders. Whoops.

An hour later, we were still all sitting in the hospital emergency room and talking when the doctor came back. He said that he'd spoken to a urologist, who wanted me to schedule a follow-up at his office the next Monday, and that I was free to go ahead and leave the hospital. He would be filling out the discharge paperwork right away, and then he left again.

I stared at the elders. "Oh my gosh, were you here when they told me I was going to have to be admitted and have a blood transfusion?"

"Yep!"

"Wow. I have no idea what you did in that blessing. It was a miracle! Thank you!"

A few months later, the mission president released his Book of Miracles. When I was first told about this, I thought, *Does this church have a book for everything? First the Book of Mormon, now the Book of Miracles. Next will it be the Book of Cooking?* He had come up with this idea when he was asked to serve in the Boston area—it is a yearly tradition for him to have all two hundred plus missionaries write a brief story describing a miracle that occurred sometime that year. Elder Christensen submitted his side of this story:

The miracle I have to share probably happened during my second week in the mission field. At the time, I was with Elder Little and I was still trying to figure the whole missionary thing out. I remember we were driving and we got a text from the sisters. They asked if we could give a blessing to one of their investigators. I had yet to pronounce a blessing or be part of one, so I was nervous but excited at the same time.

We got the address and name, and we headed there. It turned out to be a hospital. We had no idea what was going on yet, except that the investigator told the people at the front desk that when two young guys with black tags and white shirts walked in to let them come in.

At the hospital check-in, they told us we needed to wait a minute because he was having a checkup. We were outside

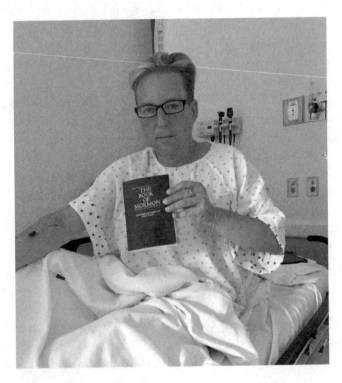

In the hospital

waiting for almost a half hour. During that time, we heard all of this screaming and wailing. Turns out it was coming from him.

They finally let us come into the room, and he just looked absolutely in pain. To keep it from being too gruesome, he was having some really bad bladder problems. We talked with him, trying to calm him down, but it wasn't helping. I was pretty nervous because he had multiple outbursts of pain. When the nurse gave us some time alone with him to give him a blessing, I sort of freaked out because I didn't really know what to do. But we trusted in the Lord and had faith that by giving this man a blessing, we could help ease his pain so he would be well enough for his baptism in seven days.

A heartfelt, Spirit-led blessing took place and in the words of the investigator: "I felt like there was no more pain and I was being lifted into heaven." That scared me, because I thought it could have been the medication he was taking. He was on a lot. But that night, he was able to leave the hospital, and he was able to get baptized.

The power of the priesthood is amazing, and I have a sure testimony of that.

The next morning, I randomly opened to this scripture in the Bible:

And when ye stand praying, forgive, if ye have ought against any: that your Father also which is in heaven may forgive you your trespasses.

But if ye do not forgive, neither will your Father which is in heaven forgive your trespasses.

And they come again to Jerusalem: and as he was walking in the temple, there come to him the chief priests, and the scribes, and the elders,

And say unto him, By what authority doest thou these things? and who gave thee this authority to do these things?

And Jesus answered and said unto them, I will also ask of you one question, and answer me, and I will tell you by what authority I do these things. (Mark 11:25–29)

I had not known before about specific priesthood authority to act in the name of God, but I certainly experienced it with the power the blessing in the hospital. This scripture reinforced what the sisters had taught me and what the elders did. I was happy and relieved that Heavenly Father would forgive all my past transgressions with my baptism, and that soon after, I would also be ordained to the priesthood and officiate in ordinances for my ancestors.

I had my interview with the mission president before church, so I pushed through the continuing pain of the previous day's fiasco to get ready. I was trying to avoid the pain medication because I didn't want to be affected by it. I know the look of someone who is high on drugs all too well, and I didn't want to do that even with prescriptions.

When I arrived at church, I was immediately introduced to the mission president. I was so nervous even though I had heard wonderful things about him from Knox and the sisters, and he was very warm and friendly. Behind closed doors, however, he was serious and stern. I later realized why. The baptismal interview is to be taken seriously, so it wasn't the time to be cool and funny. He needed to confirm that I'd been taught all the lessons prepared by the sisters, that I was following the commandments, and that I was doing the many other things that would prepare me to be baptized to become a follower of Jesus Christ.

The two of us spent about forty-five minutes talking through a series of questions, and he asked me to read various verses from the Book of Mormon. Things got real when he read from 2 Nephi and inserted my name into the verses:

"Wherefore, ye must press forward with a steadfastness in Christ, having a perfect brightness of hope, and a love of God and of all men. Wherefore, if ye shall press forward, feasting upon the word of Christ, and endure to the end, behold, thus saith the Father: Ye shall have eternal life. And now, behold, my beloved *Dennis*, this is the way; and there is none other way nor name given under heaven whereby *Dennis* can be saved in the kingdom of God. And now, behold, this is the doctrine of Christ, and the only and true doctrine of the Father, and of the Son, and of the Holy Ghost, which is one God, without end. Amen" (2 Nephi 31:20–21).

Powerful, moving, completely unexpected. It had never occurred to me to put my own name into the scriptures as if the Lord was talking to me directly. But He can, and He does! God speaks to us through the scriptures. I had chills and goosebumps all over, and I was becoming very familiar with feeling the presence of both the Holy Ghost and Darin supporting me through this important transition in my life.

The president then asked if he could invite the sisters to come in. He had not said anything either way about my baptism. I was terrified that I didn't pass, that I wasn't acceptable, that I would not be baptized.

Sister Esplin and Sister Tumlinson came in and he smiled at them, and then at me. "Congratulations! I'm all set to sign the paperwork for him to be baptized in six days."

For the first time, I felt that I finally had taken solid steps forward and that my feet were firmly planted. No more going backward.

Chapter 9

The Plunge

And straightway coming up out of the water, he saw the heavens opened, and the Spirit like a dove descending upon him:

And there came a voice from heaven, saying, Thou art my beloved Son, in whom I am well pleased.

~ Mark 1:10–11

"Wait a minute, that soon?"

I was shocked at what I heard from Andrew over the phone when I called to tell him my baptism was scheduled for August 19. Did the sister missionaries know I'm gay? Of course they did. Had I learned and did I have an understanding of what would be expected of me in this church? Yes!

Andrew sounded very urgent and concerned as he stressed to me the depth of the commitment I was making with baptism into The Church of Jesus Christ of Latter-day Saints. "If you do this, there's no going back. You're making covenants with God that you're going to do certain things for the rest of your life. This is a big deal!"

I listened but his hesitation frustrated me. What on earth? We'd switched positions. Andrew was trying to talk me *out* of being baptized? After he took me all over Palmyra and taught me the first missionary lesson in the Sacred Grove, *I* had to sell *him* on the idea of me joining the Church. This was ridiculous, so I cut him off.

"I know what this means. I know what I'm getting into. I know and realize that I can't date guys anymore. I'm going to be alone for the rest of my life, and I'm okay with that. I'm okay with it because I feel that while I'm giving up all of that, as far as I'm concerned, I'm marrying the Church."

Yes, the idea of remaining single for the rest of my life had been an obstacle to committing to baptism. I had prayed about it, and then there came a day that I had zero desire to pursue another relationship. That's the power of the Holy Ghost—it removed the yearning.

I spent quite a bit of time planning my baptism weekend with the sisters and some of the ward members, and I even obsessively made a complete itinerary for Derek and Shelby. I had asked Derek to baptize me, and Shelby to give one of the talks at the service.

Well, actually, I first asked *Shelby* to baptize me. Since I was taught by female missionaries, it didn't occur to me that women don't do all the same things as the men within the Church. Only men perform ordinances, but women definitely carry the power of God as well. The power of God is *LOVE*, and it is *women* who first exhibited the true love of God to me and brought me into this church. I am immensely grateful to Derek, Knox, Andrew, and other men for teaching me so much about the Latter-day Saint faith and helping to guide and support my path toward baptism. But it was the women who were first: Cheryl, Shelby, Audrey, Sister Guimaras in Palmyra, Sister Esplin and Sister Tumlinson in Connecticut, and so many more.

Since I couldn't make LDS history by being baptized by a woman, I did something else. I requested—and received permission from the Church leaders—to have my baptism service broadcast over Skype and for Andrew to give the opening prayer from Utah for a service being held in Connecticut.

When I emailed a draft program to Derek, he spoke to Andrew. "I've never heard of Skyping an opening prayer. Everything has to be conducted in the Church building itself. Dennis must have some incorrect information."

Andrew shrugged. "I know, but apparently he got approval from his bishop and stake president. They said we might as well start to embrace technology. It's not like we don't broadcast general conference."

Derek wasn't convinced. "Still, I've never heard of such a thing, and I'm not sure it's in accordance with our policies."

Well, I did receive permission for Andrew to do it. He was asked to be at his own Church building with his laptop and to not record anything, but he was allowed to participate through the wonders of modern technology from two thousand miles away. The next year, I was told that our stake president had requested permission from Church authorities to do it other times as well—for grandparents in convalescent homes to witness ordinances and on other occasions. He even thanked me for starting a trend.

The weekend finally arrived. It was thirty-three days since I had made that early-morning drive to Susquehanna, Pennsylvania, and my life was so, so, so different. I woke up Friday morning feeling nervous and excited, like I was getting ready for a first date, but *more*. It was so much more intense—I'd never felt that level of anticipation before.

I still had a hard time believing that Derek and Shelby were flying out from Utah at their own expense just for my baptism. I had booked a bed-and-breakfast reservation near my home for them, and I stopped by to drop off sunflowers from my grandmother's garden and a few thank you gifts before heading to the airport to pick them up.

At the other end of the country, Derek and Shelby were sitting on the runway but their flight couldn't take off because of the wind direction. There were no other flights from Salt Lake to Boston the rest of the day, and my baptism was scheduled for the next morning. So Shelby prayed. If they were to be at my baptism, God needed to make it happen. Five minutes later, they were cleared for take-off. The pilot said that other air traffic had been rerouted so their plane could get off the ground.

"It's like God was looking down at a puzzle and moved just one piece. It is that important for you to be baptized," Shelby told me when I met them at the airport. It was a very strong experience for her, and I know that God answered both of our prayers that they could be with me for such a momentous event. The glow in her face left me speechless.

When we were at dinner, Shelby pulled a bunch of gifts out of her bag, which I was not expecting. Just the fact that they had come was enough. Andrew and Audrey had sent wonderful books and multiple CDs from the Tabernacle Choir. I didn't have time to read the card or notes in the books before Shelby handed me a small box. It was a beautiful ring with the letters CTR, which stands for "Choose The Right."

"Choose the Right" is a constant reminder that has become a staple in my life. We all have the ability to choose between right and wrong, good and less good and even bad. Since receiving this ring, I wear it constantly, and it has helped remind me to use my freedom of choice in good ways. I've found myself in situations wanting to say something inappropriate, but I look at my hand and see those CTR letters. Remembering the commitment I've made to God to be a good person helps me swallow back many words that should not come out of anyone's mouth.

And that's another thing this ring helps with. Recently, I was in the temple and had the sudden thought of "Choose To Remember." Remember the Lord and all He has given to us. Remember the good times I shared with my family members whose temple work I was doing. Remember my dear friends who live so far away and the glorious times we've spent together. Remember the many blessings I continue to receive while serving our Heavenly Father and the wonderful friends I've made near and far along my journey.

The next gift was two neckties, one with the CTR logo and the other with the Angel Moroni symbol, the angel who visited Joseph Smith multiple times while he was translating the Book of Mormon.

Beginning with my visit to the Moroni statue at the Hill Cumorah, I have continued to feel a spiritual connection to him. Moroni represents strength, endurance, security, and wisdom. Through my scripture study, I have learned that Moroni wrote that the only people who can be baptized are those willing to repent of their sins and serve Jesus Christ, and if anyone loves God and follows Him, they can become more like Him.

Don't get me wrong, no one is perfect. However, we can all strive to achieve perfection in the future. We obey the commandments, serve as Jesus Christ did, and repent regularly of our sins and mistakes. Then His grace through His Atonement will make up the rest.

After all of this, well, we were in a restaurant and our food arrived. I asked Derek to offer a prayer but I had yet another lesson to learn. He explained that when in public, members of the Church usually just bow their heads quietly, say a quick prayer individually, and then eat without drawing attention to themselves. The only exception is if a person of another faith asks us to pray. I love that! I've seen too many people draw attention to their religious actions such as praying over their food in a restaurant by being showy about it, and I've never been comfortable with that. I like this way much better.

Saturday, August 19, 2017. The big day. I was wearing my new CTR tie and was all ready to jump in my car to pick up Derek and Shelby when I froze. What was going on? A panic attack? I was suddenly afraid of all of those people coming to my baptism—over half of them were not members of the Church. *What would they think of all of this? Would they still be my friends after it was done?* I have no recollection of how I made it to my car and drove to where Derek and Shelby were staying. I was completely numb.

Even though I had a lot of people attending my baptism from my company, I was very selective who I invited. I did not want people asking me, "Why are you doing this?" or "Are you nuts?" When I invited people, I made it very clear that photos were not to go on social media sites. They were not allowed to tell anyone that they were attending. This was my spiritual path, and I chose to keep it personal and quiet.

Once I saw Derek and Shelby, all fear left my body. Shelby gave me a hug, and I instantly felt safe and loved. The hustle and bustle at the church started as soon as we walked in the door. I changed right away into a funny-looking white jumpsuit as the ward members and my friends started to arrive. We took photos of Derek and me in the white clothing with the missionaries. Head spin! Everything happened very fast, and there were a lot of people around. I tried to greet everyone coming in, but there were so many. Derek advised that I wait until after the service to talk to people so that I could focus on the Holy Ghost and be mentally present with the service. He quietly talked me through how the baptism would be performed, then mutely walked me to the front of the chapel to sit down.

As I looked around the chapel, I saw so many members of the ward, old friends, members of my work team, and family. My parents did attend! They were obviously not happy about my joining this church, but I appreciated their show of support by being there. I felt like I was living two parallel but overlapping lives. Again. Instead of having relationships with other gay men, I'm now in a relationship with The Church of Jesus Christ of Latter-day Saints. My parents know about this "alternate" life, just as before, but we still don't talk about it.

I sat in the front row between Derek and Shelby with a TV monitor in front of us. The opening hymn was "I Need Thee Every Hour,"

Dennis's baptism, with Derek and the sister missionaries

a musical prayer asking the Lord to be with us always. Every minute of every day, I need the Lord's presence in my life.

Andrew really did offer the opening prayer over Skype from Utah. I still believe in my heart that he made Latter-day Saint history by being the first to do an opening prayer for a baptism over Skype. I did fold my arms and bow my head at first, but I couldn't resist opening my eyes to look up and around the chapel during the prayer. I wanted to remember my surroundings so I could recall that day for the rest of my life.

While Shelby gave the first talk, Derek just put his arm around me and held me close. What a great feeling of comfort. Wow, here was this straight man in his seventies holding onto someone who's been gay his entire life. That was so novel to me.

Many people who attended were not members of the Church and were not familiar with its doctrines, so Shelby opened her statements by explaining our basic beliefs about Heavenly Father and Jesus Christ— that They are real and we follow Them just as people from all other Christian faiths do. With baptism, we make covenants with Heavenly Father to keep His commandments, and in return, we may come into His kingdom. Shelby quoted a verse from the Book of Mormon: "And he said unto the children of men: Follow thou me. Wherefore, my beloved brethren, can we follow Jesus save we shall be willing to keep the commandments of the Father?" (2 Nephi 31:10).

Let's be honest, at this point I had been studying the Book of Mormon for only thirty days. I didn't understand everything, nor did I need to. It's not a book you read one time—you read and ponder it every day, and through constant scripture study you will gain further knowledge and insight.

I do want to follow Jesus, and I committed with my baptism to keep His commandments. I'm not perfect by any means, but I'm grateful for the ordinance of the sacrament, which Shelby also spoke about. The sacrament is a renewal of the baptismal covenant—we promise to follow the Lord, and He promises to bless us with His Spirit and allow us to return to His presence. When we make mistakes, we don't need to be rebaptized over and over to be cleansed of our sins. We take the sacrament every week to restart our path clean and rejuvenate that promise.

When Shelby completed her remarks, the entire congregation went to the back of the building where the font was. Mormons perform baptism by full immersion. The person being baptized and the person conducting the ordinance are both dressed fully in white to represent purity and cleanliness before God, and both stepped down into the water. Before we entered the font, I asked Derek to hold me under for a few seconds when he submerged me into the water so that I could fully remember the experience.

When we were in the font, I looked up and saw such a lovely group of friends and family crowded around to watch. I took a minute to make eye contact with a few people, and then Derek pronounced the baptismal prayer. Down I went, the plunge. I was warm, floating. As I was lifted back up to the air, I was lightheaded, refreshed, with a new sense of well-being and a revitalized purpose in life.

While Derek and I were changing into dry clothes, the congregation was shown a video I had selected for them. It was a segment of a talk by President Dieter F. Uchtdorf, a member of the First Presidency, titled "Our True Identity." He retells the story of "The Ugly Duckling" and urges us to reflect on who we really are—sons and daughters of a glorious Heavenly Father.

> Think of where you come from. You are sons and daughters of the greatest, most glorious being in the universe. He loves you with an infinite love. He wants the best for you. This knowledge changes everything. It changes your present, it can change your future, and it can change the world. If only we understood who we are and what is in store for us our hearts would overflow with such gratitude and happiness that it would enlighten even the darkest souls with the light and love of God.
>
> Of course there will always be voices telling you that you're foolish to believe that you're swans. Insisting that you're but ugly ducklings. And that you can't expect to become anything else. But you know better. You are no ordinary beings. You are glorious and eternal.
>
> I plead with you, just look into the water and see your true reflection. It is my prayer and blessing that when you look at your reflection you will be able to see beyond imperfections and self-doubts and recognize who you truly are: glorious sons and daughters of Almighty God.[6]

I was able to see the end of the video as I reentered the chapel, and I hoped that my friends and family would know in their hearts that they are also glorious sons and daughters of God. I also hoped that my parents were coming to feel that it's okay to have a gay son.

Immediately following the video, I received a special gift. My dear friend Bev sang "I Can Only Imagine" while her husband, John, accompanied her on the piano. Her vibrant voice carried that beautiful message of love and hope through the whole church. My head was practically in Shelby's lap as I cried and felt the presence of my beloved brother attending with us from the other side of the veil. It was significant to have this performed at my baptism because it was the catalyst that caused me to fully commit to The Church of Jesus Christ of Latter-day Saints.

My next gift was that Paula spoke after the song. She always has great stories, so I asked her to give the second talk to explain our beliefs about the Holy Ghost.

We understand that anyone can feel the Spirit of the Lord, but the gift of the Holy Ghost can only be administered by one holding priesthood of God. This constant companionship is a guide to help us through life's trials and tribulations. At Christ's baptism in the New Testament, it says that the Holy Ghost descended from heaven like a dove so that Christ could receive the Holy Ghost to be His constant companion as well. Paula is a Cub Scout leader and talks to her boys about needing to "buddy up." The Holy Ghost is how we can buddy up with the Savior to comfort us, strengthen us, and help us make correct choices in our lives.

Paula is a farmer who raises sheep, and she shared a story about how she felt God helped her when she had some crazy sheep that had gotten loose from their pasture. Her husband was ready to shrug it off and give up the sheep for lost, but Paula could picture those darned animals running all over the neighbors' lawns and ruining their landscaping. She prayed for assistance, and at random, a big truck stopped in the middle of the road. The driver also knew how to handle sheep and helped her capture the loose animals and get them back to her farm. She had asked for help, and she received it.

Paula had no idea how much this story would touch my heart. I have always considered myself the "black sheep" of my family because of all of my negative experiences, so whenever I hear anything about sheep—the regular animals or symbolically—I always pay close attention. The parallel with President Uchtdorf's video about "The Ugly Duckling" did not escape me, and I felt this was another indication from God that I am His child and that I am loved and accepted as I am.

When I was confirmed, I sat in a chair at the front of the church to have hands placed on my head and another prayer and blessing pronounced over me. I experienced the same sensation I had the week before when I received the oil blessing from the elders (minus the near-death experience)—the hair on the back of my neck stood up, and I had goosebumps all over.

As the service closed, I was able to visit with everyone who came to support me in this major life step. I took pictures with as many people as possible to add to my photo journal to remember the day. Even then, I wondered if some friends came out of plain curiosity. But I prayed that as they experienced this with me, they would understand why chose to do this.

I spent the rest of the weekend with Derek and Shelby. We went to some historical landmarks, visited with various members of the ward, and attended church services Sunday morning. It was the first time I attended church with any of my Utah colleagues, and it was delightful to experience a deeper connection with them now as brothers and sisters in Christ.

When I finally took them back to the airport, I tried to not become emotional. We gave each other big hugs, but I left quickly. As I drove home, I reflected on the past forty-eight hours and all that had happened. I wondered, *Am I going to be able to do this? Am I crazy?* I was a little lonely, but I was also elated and uplifted. And calm. I hadn't felt that calm in my entire life. The only thing I could compare it to was being submerged in the baptismal font, having all of my previous sins washed away so I was clean before God.

Chapter 10

The Wind beneath My Wings

If you can accept your differentness and learn to love it
and encourage it, then you can be someone wonderful.[7]

~ Bette Midler

I know, I know. Classic gay guy move to have a Bette Midler reference in his book. But the chapter title fits. As I went through the missionary lessons, it felt as if my spiritual life were being stuffed into one of those circus cannons and my baptism was the flashpoint of being launched into the air. I have very little foundation beneath me within the context of the Latter-day Saint faith. I don't know what will happen to me in the next life per the core Church doctrine of eternal marriage and families—that seems to be the entire purpose of the plan of salvation, and that bedrock teaching does not appear to apply to me in the slightest. As this doctrine is currently taught, eternal marriage is only for heterosexual people. I don't know if I'll still be gay in the next life, or somehow magically become straight. I don't know how it will work for me to have an eternal partner in the next life or if I will even get one. I just don't know.

I do know that God loves me and that I am His son whom He accepts without reservation. My faith in this one thing is what lifts me above the emotional storm clouds and helps me to soar through life. I have confidence that my path back to my Heavenly Father runs straight through The Church of Jesus Christ of Latter-day Saints. I hold on to these two things with all of my heart and soul, and I receive continual reassurance from the Holy Ghost that I'm doing the right thing for my own life.

Don't get me wrong—I am not in any way cruising smoothly at a high altitude. There is a lot of turbulence every day to throw me around and make me feel like I'm in free fall, and it's terrifying. It's when I relax and trust God to hold me up with His powerful air currents that I'm lifted higher spiritually.

Another manifestation of God's air currents keeping me up is the people of the Church. From what I read online prior to my baptism, this is not usually the case. So many LGBT people have been rejected by their Latter-day Saint families, leaders, and wards just because of their sexual orientation, but that has not been the situation for me. I have been welcomed, supported, and loved by both my long-distance friends and my local ward and stake. I have never felt judged in their arms for my orientation. It shouldn't matter if you're Caucasian, purple, African American, Asian, gay, questioning, Democrat, Republican, or Independent. When we get a paper cut, everyone bleeds red. My mantra is "Let's turn up the love!"

Two months after my baptism, I was traveling for a little vacation, visiting friends and fellow people within my team. On my journey home, I was delighted to meet a fellow LGBT member of the Church for dinner in Virginia. My mind raced with thousands of questions I wanted to ask John. The first one was to clarify that he is indeed gay and an active member of the Church of Jesus Christ.

"I joined the Church almost thirty years ago as an openly gay convert and have always believed in the restored gospel," he told me. "That's not to say I haven't stepped away sometimes, but I always find my way back to living the standards and holding a temple recommend."

We sat in a quiet section of a restaurant, and I hoped he would never stop talking. I could have sat there with him for days. He shared many positive stories, his experiences doing temple work, and the blessings he has received through his priesthood leaders. It was exactly what I needed to hear so I could know and affirm that there are others like me. We have stayed in touch through social media and talk on the phone regularly. He has continued to be a supportive friend through the many ups and downs of life.

Back to back with my trip through the South, I needed to go to Utah for a business convention. I was overjoyed at the prospect of spending time with my dear friends who had helped me learn about this wonderful religious community. The convention was in Salt Lake City. I first went to St. George in southern Utah to spend a couple of days with Derek and Shelby in their home.

As soon as I entered their house, I felt like I was at home with my own family. I hadn't had that feeling in such a long time, and it took some getting used to. These two beautiful souls had dropped everything to fly to the East Coast for my baptism—how could I not feel at home with them? We did some sight-seeing, and I met some of their family over the next couple of days. I was enthralled the entire time. I truly feel as though they are a second set of parents for me, who love and accept me with no conditions. There is no "but" attached to anything.

At our national convention with Zija International, I was enthusiastic as I reconnected with my team, more company leadership, and the corporate office staff who makes things happen behind the scenes. It was a very different feeling for me compared to other conventions. They were always enjoyable. They were always fulfilling. But now, instead of meeting with colleagues, I was meeting with colleagues who were *also* brothers and sisters in my religious faith. Work and church blended a lot more. I didn't sit with my team and have wine. Now I was sitting with the company owners and drinking lemonade.

People could tell something was different. I was questioned many times—"What's changed? You have this glow or aura about you." I just replied, "Business is doing great!"

I felt more complete because of the Church connection, but I wasn't ready to make a grand announcement to my team and colleagues that I had been baptized. Now that I think about it, I was lying at that convention, and it brings back memories of being a closeted gay. Now I was a closeted Mormon! My business had actually started to unravel a bit because I spent so much of my time and energy on my Latter-day Saint studies. I had stopped recruiting, stopped working with the leaders in my downline, and therefore they stopped working with their teams. It was a trickle-down effect. I couldn't bring myself to share this with anyone, so I just kept up the persona that everything is great. Don't get me wrong—everything was great in a spiritual and religious aspect. But my business was definitely taking a beating. The convention was a great motivator for my business, and I was ready to get back to work as soon as I returned to Connecticut.

But first I had some other things to do in Utah. I had been to Utah a few times before, but I'd never paid attention to anything other than the gorgeous mountains. My perception was that the people there were extremely homophobic and racist. I would tell my assistant booking the flights to get me out of there as quickly as possible. This time, however, I didn't want to leave.

After the convention ended on a Sunday morning, Andrew and Audrey were going with me for my first visit to Temple Square and to hear the Tabernacle Choir perform live. We were joined by another couple from the company I knew vaguely. Earlier in the week, they had gone to Deseret Book, the Church-owned bookstore, and purchased a copy of the Book of Mormon, not realizing that they could get it for free from the missionaries. When they had approached Andrew to ask him questions about the LDS Church, he immediately referred them to me as I was so recently baptized. They were so surprised—they had no clue.

I was so elated to answer their questions that I committed every network marketer's worst nightmare: I rambled, rather than asking questions and listening. In this case, it didn't matter as much. They felt the spirit of Temple Square and were also excited to see the Tabernacle Choir perform. It was an enchanting experience to be there. I truly felt I was in Shangri-La.

Ten minutes before the choir was to go live, a woman addressed the audience to explain what was about to occur, as *Music and the Spoken Word* is the oldest and longest running show in recording history. We were told to turn off all cell phones, as the Tabernacle was designed with amazing acoustics. You can hear the drop of a pin on the podium even at the back of the auditorium. Before it went live, we were instructed to try not cough or sneeze and to please not drop anything. Two minutes into the live broadcast, the Moroni pin on the lapel of my jacket decided to pop off and fall to the floor. I was sitting on the end of the row, and the five of us just stared at each other. I was so mortified but threw my hands up and pretended nothing had happened. Only me! After the broadcast, I explained what had happened and we were laughing so hard. "That's our Dennis! He's a very unique character!"

We crossed the street to the Conference Center, a massive auditorium built specifically to host general conference. General conference is a semiannual event in which the main General Authorities speak to the entire population of the Church and anyone else who cares to listen. It is broadcast live all over the world via the internet and TV satellites, and Mormons everywhere listen to the sermons. The conferences are archived online for decades—you can watch general conference videos online dating clear back to 1971.

I was surprised that the Conference Center was open on a Sunday, but there were volunteers offering tours. So we spent an hour and a half listening to the history of how the center was built and completed in the year 2000. The building houses a three-tiered platform with no structural beams that seats over 21,000 people, and engineers come from around the world to marvel at its unique structure.

Our guide took us to the roof, where there are streams and waterfalls, mountain plants and deserts. She said the foliage was designed to look like the United States of America—we started on the East Coast, made our way to the Midwest and the Rocky Mountains, and ended on the West Coast. They had everything from New England's maple trees to spruce trees more prevalent at higher elevations.

We continued around Temple Square to the two visitors' centers and the reflection pool at the base of the Salt Lake Temple. Andrew was clicking away with his camera the entire time, and I am so blessed to have those photos. The volunteers were the perfect tour guides, and they knew the history of the Church inside and out. They had answers to all my questions.

We left Salt Lake City to go to Provo for a few more days. Andrew wanted to show me the big Y painted halfway up the mountain overlooking Brigham Young University. We did some hiking, took a ton of photos (of course), and walked around the BYU campus. I was shocked to see we were the only people at this large university—it was like a ghost town. It was a Sunday afternoon, so there were no classes scheduled, but I didn't think it would be so completely vacant.

I was dying of thirst, so when we stopped to take a break, I found a vending machine. I inserted a dollar but the machine spit it back out. So

I used my credit card—not accepted. Another card—not accepted . . . I was starting to get nervous that I was a victim of credit card fraud when Andrew realized what was happening.

"It's Sunday. They turn off the machines. We're not supposed to buy anything unless it's an emergency."

I thought that was a hoot. "Well, it's an emergency! I have cotton mouth from all the walking and I'm dehydrated!" I guess when you're in a state that's majority Latter-day Saints, nothing is open on Sunday. I must admit, it reminds me of "the good ole days" when stores were not open on Sundays. It's supposed to be a day of rest. Somehow, as large conglomerates, corporations, and retailers become more money-hungry, the rest of the world has forgotten that. I'm now in a community that is not like that. We live the gospel not only on the Sabbath but also during the other six days of the week.

We went to Audrey's parents' home, where I met all of Audrey's family *and* Andrew's parents and sister. It was like Thanksgiving with everyone gathered for a holiday. It was two days before Halloween, and the house was decked out. Even the place settings had black and yellow plates, cutlery in the shape of skeletons, and spiders wrapped around the stemware. It was like I was at Disneyland touring the Haunted House. And it wasn't just the inside of their house decorated, either. Outside, it was like there was a contest that every house in the neighborhood had to be festooned to the nines. I later mentioned to Andrew, "Holy cow, you guys take holidays seriously!" I didn't think the Mormons even celebrated Halloween.

Everyone knew everything about me, and I knew nothing about them. My palms were sweaty as I was greeting everyone and learning their names, but I was soon blown away by their kindness. During and after dinner, the camaraderie and conversation just kept flowing. I still couldn't comprehend how hospitable, warm, and kind these families were from the minute we were introduced. They were willing to make me a part of their own family based only on what they had heard from Andrew. I get choked up now just thinking about it.

I was staying that night in the in-law suite of the home, and Audrey's mom, Judy, went out of her way to make sure I was comfortable. She even placed mints and chocolates on the pillow and made sure I had a refrigerator full of food along with some microwave popcorn. Judy invited me to accompany her to a Zumba class the next morning.

As we were driving to the class, Judy caught me off guard. "Dennis, I've never known any gay people before you. I always thought it was a choice. After meeting you, my heart goes out to you, as I definitely feel the challenges you had throughout your life. I will try to bear your burdens along your side. I now realize that you did not choose to be gay, and I am so sorry for my ignorance."

I was speechless for a few minutes as I just grabbed her hand and squeezed it. I'd already been told many times that Mormons in Utah live in a bubble, and this seemed to validate that stereotype. But it seemed to be overcome so easily. All it took was for Judy to spend a little bit of time with me, ask a few questions about LGBT, and listen, and then she accepted.

I finally said the only thing that came to mind. "It's not ignorance. It's innocence and a lack of understanding. I don't need to be known as 'This is my gay friend Dennis who's LDS.' You can just refer to me as Dennis. If it happens to come up, then yes, I'm gay, and yes I'm Mormon. One of the biggest compliments you can get is if one of your LGBT friends comes out to you. Be that person. Lay the foundation of kindness and inclusiveness now so they will open up later. Think about 'What would Jesus do?'"

I'm just Dennis. Who happens to be LDS. And happens to be gay.

I was so happy to expand my "extended family" in Utah through Andrew and Audrey's family. But the highlight of the entire trip was what I did for my biological family. Andrew and I went to the Provo City Center Temple with Audrey and his sister, Amy, to perform vicarious baptisms in behalf of my beloved brother, Darin, and some other ancestors.

I had previously done proxy baptisms for the dead at the Hartford Connecticut Temple with Sister Tumlinson and Sister Esplin shortly after my own baptism. But I saved Darin's name for a special occasion since he was the major influence in my revelation to join the Church. What better time than when I was in Utah and Andrew could baptize me in Darin's behalf.

The moment I walked through the temple doors, scanned my recommend at the desk, and started making my way down the hall to the baptistry, I was suddenly overcome with the feeling that Darin was right there in the temple with me. Between sensing both Darin's and the Holy Ghost's presence, I couldn't contain myself. So many overwhelming emotions were unleashed, resulting in me hyperventilating and sobbing uncontrollably until I entered the baptismal font.

The Provo City Center Temple baptistry is a cream-colored room with dark wood trim around the doors and windows. There are a couple of paintings on the wall depicting Jesus Christ's baptism by John the Baptist. A wood rail surrounds the stone font, which rests on the backs of twelve metallic, gray oxen. It is a beautiful, quiet, peaceful place. But the beauty of the temple does not compare to the beauty of the ordinances performed in it: being baptized in behalf of my deceased family members to provide them with the opportunity to choose for themselves if they will follow Christ in the eternities and live in the presence of our Heavenly Parents as a family for forever.

After Andrew and I changed into the white jumpsuits, we sat peacefully by the font. Other people were speaking quietly around me,

Darin's baptism at the Provo City Center Temple

but I was having a conversation with my brother in my head. *Darin, this is your day. I wouldn't be here if it wasn't for you.*

Andrew went into the font first, and he baptized Audrey and Amy in behalf of some of my female ancestors. As they began, one of the temple workers approached where I was sitting to wait. "Brother, this is a very important day for you. Why don't you stand up by the font so you can have a better view and be closer to your family?"

My voice cracked as I thanked him and went to the rail at the edge of the font to watch as the baptisms were performed. Even now as I write this, a tear is running down my cheek at the memory of that moment.

When it was my turn, I took my time descending into the warm water, looking around and noticing the details. Can I remember it all now? Not completely. I remember sensing that Darin was in the temple with us. I remember tingles all over my body. I remember peace. I remember the water of the font blending with my tears so I didn't know which was which.

For me personally, I had not previously experienced a validating feeling during the baptism ordinance that my ancestors had accepted it or not. It has happened afterward during the proxy confirmation—when their names are read for the confirmation of the gift of the Holy Ghost, I feel goosebumps. This time, with Darin, it was goosebumps, chills, and many tears.

Remember, we all have the ability to choose, and that freedom does not end in this life. Darin has the choice to accept or reject the baptism I did in his behalf, and I undeniably believe he accepted it.

Once we were outside walking on the temple grounds, Andrew pulled out his camera to shoot some photos. I've learned that, like me, he always wants to capture important moments like this day was for me. Going through them now, I have to laugh because I look like I'd been hit by a truck. I remember thinking, *Come on, Andrew, seriously? Now? You have to take pictures NOW?* After a few minutes of taking photos, I wanted to absorb what had just happened in the baptistry and reflect on the experience without the camera. At the time, I just wanted a moment alone to marvel over the spirit of the temple and doing work for our kindred dead. But now, looking back, I'm grateful for those photos. They're part of my diary, and I will cherish those memories forever.

Chapter 11

Opposition in All Things

You gain strength, courage, and confidence by every experience in which you really stop to look fear in the face.

You are able to say to yourself, "I lived through this horror. I can take the next thing that comes along."[8]

~ Eleanor Roosevelt

There's a saying that becoming a member of The Church of Jesus Christ of Latter-day Saints is not a guarantee that all your troubles will go away, but you will have the Holy Ghost to help you deal with them.

We all have challenges to our faith and beliefs, in our jobs and education, with our friends and family—everywhere. Converts in particular can run into severe questioning when they change old habits and replace them with different, more strict standards.

I was on location at an event as a lifestyle reporter when my producer became upset that I wouldn't taste-test for a local coffee shop. It wasn't an appropriate time to go into details about the Word of Wisdom, so I just said, "It's religious."

He rolled his eyes. "Oh, great. That means you're not going to do the wine and beer tastings now?"

I didn't know what to do, so I agreed to act the wine-tasting for the filming, as long as the glass had white cranberry juice in it. I was very disconcerted but didn't know what else to do. I was apprehensive that people from my ward would see the episode. It had been only one month since my baptism, and it would look like I was already reverting to my former patterns.

I called Andrew to get advice for how to handle things if something similar happened again in the future. He patiently listened and wasn't upset with what I had done. We talked about a concept I wasn't familiar with—avoiding the appearance of evil. I was unsettled because I *appeared* to be breaking a commandment even though I actually wasn't. This makes so much sense to me now.

Then Andrew's voice started rising in volume and pitch. At first, this frightened me a little. I thought, *Holy stars, what did I do?* But Andrew wasn't angry at all, he was beaming. "I couldn't be happier or more proud of who you've become."

"Andrew, what?! Why?"

"Just knowing that you're worried about this, along with hearing the concern in your voice, shows me that you have grown so much. In a very short time, your life indisputably has undergone a 360-degree turn. And your friends in Utah have a front-row seat witnessing your transformation. Most people would have shrugged this off like it was no big deal. You, on the other hand, made my day."

He then went on to make a great marketing suggestion. "With so many people at these events, you could easily pull someone from the audience and ask them if they would like to taste the beer or wine, and share their thoughts with the reviewers." He's a genius!

With a little bit of guidance, I can handle challenges like this in my life. I can deal with the lack of support from my family and friends who are members of other churches. But Satan plays a mean mind game before you're baptized, and it gets even worse after you're baptized.

For months, I questioned a lot whether I'd made the right decision to be baptized into The Church of Jesus Christ of Latter-day Saints. Even now, my inner monologues are incredibly dramatic as I fight off the adversary to stay in the Church and keep my commitments to God. If you allow him, the adversary will take full control and overcome your thought processes with his own warped reality.

So often, I have thought, *I just can't handle this anymore! Why me, God? Have I lost my mind? Maybe I really am nuts.*

Hesitation and doubt are legitimate feelings to have, but what you do next is the challenge. I've learned that the best response is, *What do I need to learn from this? All of this is happening for a reason to help me become a stronger person inside and out.*

The February after my baptism, I was called to the bishop's office during church. My immediate thought was, *Oh heavens, did I do something wrong?* I couldn't think of anything I had done recently that was outside the bounds of what I'd been taught by the sisters, but why else would someone be called in to talk to the bishop?

The bishop is not like the principal of a school. He's not there to get you in trouble. "Everything's fine. I just want to interview you to receive the Melchizedek Priesthood."

"What? Wow, that's so soon!" I wasn't even sure if I knew what the Melchizedek Priesthood meant or what I would be allowed to do once I was ordained.

I was asked all the typical questions about my worthiness and whether I was following the gospel teachings. We shared some spiritual success stories, and he told me how happy he was that I was progressing within the Church. "The Church needs you."

I struggled with accepting that a little bit. I didn't want this to be about me; I wanted it to be about what I could give to others. "Thank you. I need the Church too."

I was definitely on cloud nine when I texted friends in Utah to tell them the news. I also asked Knox and John, my LGBT convert friends, how soon they had received the Melchizedek Priesthood after joining the Church, and they both said it was over a year after their baptisms.

I ended the day with a natural buzz from all the encouragement and support flowing through my phone in text messages from friends and colleagues in Utah. The Holy Ghost was with me as I prayed and went to bed for an extremely peaceful and restful night's sleep.

Bam. The next morning, I woke up into a dark mental cloud that paralyzed me with fear. *You're not worthy. You don't deserve this. It's too soon. You're gay, and that's what's wrong with you. You are not of God, and your church hates gays. This isn't what they believe in.*

These thoughts persisted for a few days. Every time I picked up the phone to call the stake president to complete my interview process for the priesthood, the dark cloud would take over my mind again. *You're not worthy! You don't deserve this! It's wrong to be gay!* I would put the phone back down without making the call. I tried to pray it away, and finally I was on my knees pleading with God for mercy, for some kind of outside help, when the phone rang. It was the sister missionaries with an investigator I had met with a couple of times, asking me to baptize her.

"Oh my heavens! Of course, I couldn't be more honored!" That was my answer. The mental black cloud dissipated, and I immediately called the stake president to schedule my Melchizedek Priesthood interview. I apologized for not calling sooner and explained my challenge with the adversary. He gave me so much encouragement and reassured me that I was living my life according to my covenants with God. What an awesome man. We've always clicked. He gets me. He listens, learns, and loves even more.

Roadblocks, challenges, trials, tribulations—whatever you want to call them, we're all going to have them. It's a fact of life. It's what we do when we're faced with them that matters. We can give up and be defeated. Or we can use them to grow and become stronger. I believe and know in my heart that God is there for every one of us. I pray and tell God, "I need your help right now!" When I don't know the answer to a question, I ask the Holy Ghost. They want to help us.

Fast-forward to the summer of 2018. I was on the phone with my bishop, helping him counsel another member who was having a personal crisis. One of his counselors was concerned that I was too green (a term used to describe new missionaries in the field), and this might cause me to lose my testimony. Nope. It's so much easier for me to handle adversity when someone else is in crisis. I perk up, immerse myself in assisting them any way I can, and make sure they're feeling my undivided attention. I can put my own challenges to the side when I'm focusing on other people. I can say in my mind, *Lucifer, be gone! I have members in the Church that need me, Satan. I do not have time for you now, bye-bye!*

Chapter 12

Called to Serve

Wherefore, how great the importance to make these
things known unto the inhabitants of the earth, that
they may know that there is no flesh that can dwell in
the presence of God, save it be through the merits, and
mercy, and grace of the Holy Messiah, who layeth down
his life according to the flesh, and taketh it again by
the power of the Spirit, that he may bring to pass the
resurrection of the dead, being the first that should rise.

~ 2 Nephi 2:8

As the sisters and elders transferred throughout the stake and mission,
the news spread fast that an openly gay man in Connecticut was baptized into the Church.

Around the same time I was going through the mental drama
about receiving the Melchizedek Priesthood, I received a call from the
sister missionaries in Hartford, asking if I would go to a discussion at
the home of one of their investigators. I asked what the purpose was,
and they told me they had someone investigating the Church who had
concerns about LGBT issues.

The sisters and I met at the investigator's home one afternoon, and
they told me a little bit about Jackie before we went inside. We sat in

her living room, and the sisters started their lesson. While they were teaching, a feeling came over me that this woman was going to be baptized. Now that's the Holy Ghost! I interrupted the sisters and said to Jackie, "You've been investigating our church for four and a half years. You gave up drinking coffee, smoking cigarettes, and drinking alcohol, all to join the LDS faith. I'm going to be bold, Jackie. I'm going to use a typical network marketing term to determine a level of interest on your part. On a scale of one to ten—one, meaning you want the sisters and me to run for the door and never look back; ten, you're willing to be baptized tomorrow—what number are you?"

Her reply was honest. "Seven point two."

"Great! What questions could I answer that would bring you to an eight today?"

"Well, I have some concerns with the Church's stance on LGBT issues. I have friends who are gay, lesbian, and transgender, and I don't want to join an organization that hates and doesn't accept them."

"That's a good question. First, I would like to clarify that although we are a religious organization, I see it more as a family. I'll be honest with you. In the past, we've had a reputation of being accepting but not fully allowing our gay and lesbian brothers and sisters to be in good standing with the Church. However! We are a church of prophecy and revelation. We believe in the restored Church of Jesus Christ. We have a living prophet and twelve Apostles in an organizational structure that uses prayer to determine the Church's outcome. We believe that they are directed by God. There have been some amazing changes that they've unfolded in the last couple of years. For example, they launched a website, MormonAndGay.org, with videos, scriptures, and testimonials from our LGBT brothers and sisters along with their family members. I did not choose to be gay, but I did choose to be baptized into the LDS faith and get confirmed to receive the Holy Ghost. That has been the most amazing experience in my forty-five years of living. I wouldn't want to live without it." I paused. "Now what number are you?"

"I'm an eight point five!"

"That's awesome, Jackie! With next week's teaching visit, the sisters are going to bring you to a nine, and then we're going to fast and pray together to come up with a baptismal date."

After the appointment, we texted a little, and I sent her some videos. We talked on the phone a few times, and I let the sister missionaries do what they were trained to do.

My second meeting with Jackie was to schedule her baptism. When we arrived, there was a very unsettled feeling—she must have been dealing with her own adversary. No one knew how this went better than I did. I'm not sure what I said during that lesson, but by the end, Jackie was calm and ready to go forward with the baptism commitment. She scheduled her interview with the mission leader, and I worked with the sisters to make all the plans and schedules so that the baptism day would run smoothly. The sisters continued to teach Jackie everything she needed to know ahead of the most life-changing and rewarding event in her life. Watching it all unfold from the outside was almost like watching myself! After all, it was not so long ago that this had been my life. I couldn't wait for Jackie's baptism. I was so excited for her to feel what I felt in the font on my baptism day: nothing but love.

That was the first of many, many discussions I have attended with missionaries around the entire New England region. As the Hartford missionaries transferred to other places, they continued to call me to accompany them to lessons down on the shoreline, in the Boston area, and in Rhode Island. I was asked to share my personal story of coming into the Church in an effort to help others possibly find their own path to conversion. I have been blessed to baptize some of these people as well, starting with Jackie.

The day of her baptism was also stake conference. With all the emotional tribulations that week leading up to just *scheduling* my Melchizedek Priesthood interview, I still didn't feel worthy enough to perform the baptism and wanted to be clean from all sins that day. I had done nothing to make me unworthy, but I still had a burning desire to receive the sacrament prior to the baptism.

When stake conference occurs, however, the sacrament is not administered that day. I was housesitting in another part of the state for some friends, so before going home to attend stake conference and Jackie's baptism, I stopped in a ward near my friends' home to receive the sacrament.

Because I was late for stake conference, my phone was blowing up with texts from Jackie and the sister missionaries. "Where are you?

Mission President Miller is here and wants to meet with you." My mind was racing in all directions, including a nefarious little thought that I *still* wasn't worthy to go forward with any of this. But I completed the sacrament ordinance and raced to stake conference. Oh, and to top it off, my first thought was, *What did I do now that President Miller needs to see me?* It's funny where your mind goes when you're mentally exhausted from weeks of dealing with the adversary playing games and tricks.

To add to the excitement of the day, there was a General Authority visiting from Salt Lake City. When the services ended, I was able to meet him for a short time. I blurted out that I was a new gay convert and started sharing my conversion story with him. Who does that right off the bat? It was seriously time to buy a muzzle for myself.

He was very kind and put his hand on my shoulder. He told me in a subsequent conversation that as we talked then, he powerfully felt our Heavenly Father's and our Savior's love for me and that They rejoiced in the choices I was making in my life to live the gospel in its fulness.

"Dennis, you need the Church, and the Church needs you. We love you! Your Heavenly Father and your Savior love you, and I know They are grateful for your faithfulness and willingness to keep Their commandments. It may not be easy and not everyone will understand, but you can help a lot of people. What do your gay friends say when you tell them you're LDS?"

Nervousness suddenly came over me. I wasn't completely "out" as a Mormon to my friends of other faiths. The few I had shared it with had serious reservations and had reacted very negatively, dissuading me from sharing my news further. "Are you nuts?" they would say. "Have you completely lost your mind? You're joking! That is the most homophobic, racist, antifeminist church! You've joined a cult! They're only using you to try to make you straight."

But now, this General Authority smiled and gave me a hug, encouraging me to tell my story and share it with others, and reminding me that Heavenly Father and Jesus Christ love me unconditionally. I've grown to accept this more fully since that very first conversation with Shelby when she said, "Jesus *does* love you." It's still wonderful to receive continual reassurance of that through Church leaders.

Since you are reading this book, I obviously followed this suggestion to share my conversion experience. That encouragement planted a seed in my mind that the Holy Ghost pushed for quite a while: "Write a book!" But I didn't want to face ridicule from the LGBT community or members of the Church. I didn't want to be perceived as someone trying to change the Church, or that I joined the Church to write a conversion book and profit from it. I also didn't feel ready to share my personal story with such a broad audience as, well, the whole world.

But we'll deal with that later. I had no time to digest any of it because I was immediately whisked away by the sister missionaries to baptize Jackie.

I was so happy to see the mission president who had done my own interview to be baptized. He gave me a huge hug, lifting me entirely off the floor and saying, "You're doing some amazing work!" He provided some tips for my first baptism. When someone is baptized, there are two witnesses to make sure the prayer is said word perfect and that the person being baptized is completely submerged. I guess there's nothing like having to do the prayer and dunk multiple times. That's a lot of plunging.

On to the meeting that the sisters mentioned. As it turns out, I had nothing to worry about with the mission president—he only wanted show me a few techniques and personally thank me for all the sisters and elders I've been doing home teachings with. He assured me that I was filling a gap as well giving the missionaries a breath of fresh air and helping them share the gospel.

I was so excited about performing my first baptism that I thought I would forget what to say, so I typed out the prayer on a large sheet of paper. I wanted everyone in the room to hear, so I shouted. Whoops! The tile in the baptismal font creates an echo chamber—you could hear me all over the building. Well, on the bright side, at least everyone felt the vibration!

On my way home, I received a rather unexpected call. It was a friend of mine who also happened to be a friend in the Church from Salt Lake. When I say the call was unexpected, I mean he threw me for a loop. He suggested that I write a book about my conversion story. I had *never* considered this before, so my initial instinct was to say no. But he mentioned that during his service for the Church he has seen work wonders with people. Stories like mine. I told him that I ᵕᵤᵤ think about it.

In the coming days, the thought returned about writing a book of my conversion story. I had previous experience with the publishing industry—writing and publishing a book is not something to be done on a whim. Most authors don't make any money at all compared to the effort expended, so this was certainly not a get-rich-quick scheme.

For the next few days, I put up a lot of resistance to the nagging Holy Ghost. I pondered and prayed. I didn't feel ready to share my personal story—it's so sacred to me! Every time I prayed, I was told, "You can do this. Make it happen, you've got this!" But I pushed back. Yep, way to go, Dennis. Ignoring the Holy Ghost repeatedly. That's the complete opposite of what we're taught to do. If you get an impression from the Holy Ghost, don't ever ignore it.

Another concern, besides putting myself out before the world, was that I'm dyslexic. I use voice recognition software to dictate all of my emails and texts, but there's no guarantee it will actually type what you intended to say. Technical difficulties are common and frequent. I eventually realized that I was my own worst enemy, and I just started dictating into my computer. You can achieve anything you put your mind to, if you are willing to put in the effort. If you have a dream of being a published author but have a handicap, there are ways around everything. Set goals, follow them, and make it happen.

Because I've worked many years within the publishing industry, I was not concerned about finding an agent to market the book. I have many contacts. I was worried, however, about which companies the book might be marketed to. What if it went to a mainstream publishing house with an acquisitions team that knows nothing about The Church of Jesus Christ of Latter-day Saints? Once a contract is signed, they would be within their rights to sensationalize things, delete crucial information relevant to the LDS faith, or change and delete anything they want. I thought that there couldn't possibly be an Church-owned publisher, but of course there are several.

When I was in Upstate New York and we were driving to Niagara Falls, Audrey had shown me a book: *More than the Tattooed Mormon* by Al Carraway. She was so enthusiastic about it. She said, "You have to read this book. You're going to *love* her!" Remember that I was still fairly new to even learning about the Church at this time. I took the

book and said something like, "Wow, that's nice! Thanks for sharing!" That's what I said, but what I was thinking to myself was, *Why
on earth would I want to read about a tattooed Mormon? Besides, I'm
scared of needles—I don't have tattoos. What could I possibly learn from
this woman?*

After we got home from that trip, Audrey would bring Al
Carraway's book up in conversation constantly. When I was on the
phone with her or we would exchange a few texts, she would inevita-
bly ask me if I bought Al's book. Her husband even sent me a ton of
YouTube videos featuring Al that I ignored. Audrey was so enthusiastic and I didn't want to burst her bubble. So I was polite. I told her the
truth: I had decided to focus all of my studies on the scriptures right
now and other words of the prophets. I was still so new. It felt like
there was so much to learn and not enough time to do it in.

Then one day I get a phone call from Audrey's mom. She said,
"You have to read Al's book. She just came out with a revised edition.
Seriously! Let me order one for you."

Now her mom *is calling me and offering to buy me her book?!* Not
only does our Church give away books for free, but the members also
have that habit!

"Okay, okay, I get it! Tomorrow I have a two-hour drive. I'm meeting missionaries for home teaching with another person who's concerned about our stance on LGBT issues. I'll download the book on
iTunes and listen to it while I drive."

The next day rolls around. It's the end of May, a gorgeous day,
temperature in the seventies, not a cloud in the sky. I'm driving down
the parkway listening to this woman share her story and I am going,
"Holy cow!" We're not talking one farm from the West Coast—I
now had hundreds of cattle ranches hitting me upside the head. This
remarkable woman was telling *my* story. I couldn't stop listening to
every word! It resonated with my own experience of resistance, then
acceptance, and also tolerance from other people within the world
we live. And then, a quiet thought and assurance came to my mind:
*This has to be without a doubt an LDS publishing house. I'm going to be
published by them, and Sister Carraway is going to write my foreword.* It
couldn't have been clearer than the beautiful sky.

How does this tie in with all the missionaries calling me? I was now
being called by missionaries all over New England whenever they were

teaching someone who was LGBT, had concerns about LGBT issues, or had a lack of knowledge about God's love for all people. I even visited people who left the Church and still believe in the Book of Mormon but have problems with Church policies regarding LGBT people.

Missionary work is a wonderful way to serve, but it was also a bit selfish of me. To cope with my own personal challenges, I immersed myself in the service of helping the sisters, elders, and ward members as often as possible. It's my only true hiding spot from the adversary.

The missionaries around Hartford definitely kept my schedule full. In the spring, the sisters contacted a man who had relocated to New England from the Midwest and had requested a free copy of the Book of Mormon from Mormon.org. Pete had been searching for spiritual fulfillment and believed in everything he read about The Church of Jesus Christ of Latter-day Saints with the exception of one thing: he's gay, and he does not like the Church's views or policies on LGBT people. So the sisters called me. Because the missionaries are young and often have rarely interacted with LGBT individuals, it is helpful for someone like me to be put in front of a potentially interested party so I can share my testimony of the love that Heavenly Father and Jesus Christ have for all Their children. I always pray that people will feel the Holy Ghost through my testimony, as He is the one who touches hearts.

We had to reschedule twice, and then we were gearing up for a large snowstorm. It was late March, come on! All I could do was pray that the snow would hold off until after our meeting. When we arrived at the door, Pete was surprised. "Wow, there are so many of you!"

When the sisters introduced me as a gay convert, he looked knowingly at them. "Oh, now I see where this is going."

I asked him what his concerns are. He had already done so much research into our beliefs and had even called the Church to get a free copy of the Book of Mormon, so what was holding him back?

Pete wanted to adopt children. But the Church announced in 2015 that children of gay couples were not allowed to be baptized at the age of eight, which is the typical age for children in the Church, and would have to wait until they were adults.

I said, "By the time you go through the adoption process, it could be ten or twelve years from now before your children are eight. We're a church of prophecy and revelation, and things are constantly changing. Maybe that will change. On April 4, 2019, the Church announced that children of parents who identify themselves as lesbian, gay, bisexual, or transgender may now be blessed as infants and baptized in The Church of Jesus Christ of Latter-day Saints without First Presidency approval.

In addition, the Church will no longer characterize same-gender marriage by a Church member as "apostasy."

Pete, why would you want to miss out on ten or twelve years of blessings you could be receiving through the help of the Holy Ghost?"

He was really moved by that, and the sisters were able to schedule a follow-up visit. Unfortunately, his information was lost during mission transfers for a lengthy time, and the missionaries only recently established contact with him again.

Shortly before the one-year anniversary of my baptism, I received a call from Sister Tumlinson, who had walked me through my own initial covenants. It turns out it was her birthday, and she was being released to go home the following day. But on her last day in the field, she asked if I'd visit in her new area to talk with someone who had been investigating the Church for quite a long time and hesitated about baptism because of the Church's position on LGBTs. This is a recurring theme.

My favorite thing about missionary work is that I'm always meeting wonderful and amazing people. Michelle was no exception. At first, she was taken aback as to why the sisters brought a random person with them to her meeting. When she found out I'm gay, she said the same thing as Pete: "Oh, now I see where this is going." And I asked what her concerns were.

She said, "I have many gay friends, and I feel that I would be letting them down or that they would think of me differently if they found out I became Mormon. I've been studying the Church for many years and believe everything they stand for with the exception of the policies on LGBT people. I can't stand behind and support a church that doesn't allow my friends the same rights I have as a heterosexual woman. I didn't choose to be straight, but I do have the choice to join and support your church."

I gave her a smile. "Great point. I'm usually the one in that analogy. I didn't choose to be gay, but I did choose to be baptized into the LDS Church. It's great to hear that from someone like you. I commend you for your support for our LGBT brothers and sisters.

There's one thing I want to say, though. There are a lot of things happening within the LDS Church to provide common ground for all of us. There are a lot of things about the Church that don't come up in a Google search. It often only shows the negative and not the positive." I then shared my testimony along with blessings I've received since joining the Church.

I felt compelled to offer her a priesthood blessing of comfort, and she accepted. Later, she told me that she felt something during the blessing that she had never experienced before: the presence and power of the Holy Ghost. When we are prepared spiritually and have prayed before missionary discussions and lessons, we can be a conduit of God's power to other people. It never fails.

Chapter 13

I'm Out

That you may be equal in the bonds of heavenly things,
yea, and earthly things also, for the obtaining of
heavenly things. For if ye are not equal in earthly things
ye cannot be equal in obtaining heavenly things.

~ Doctrine and Covenants 78:5–6

I was convinced that my days of "coming out" were many years ago. I came out in 1990 by appearing on a national talk show, and I came out again in 2006 with the publication of my book about having an affair with a married man whose wife wasn't aware he was gay. With those troublesome times behind me, I never thought I'd have to "come out" again. Well . . . never say never.

Saturday night, May 5, 2018, I had a strong urge to share my testimony in sacrament meeting the next day. In particular, I needed to tell my ward that I'm gay. *Wait, what?* I already had a pattern of speaking in testimony meeting every month. Why did this time need to be so dramatically different? *There's no way! I'm not doing this!*

The thought wouldn't leave. I fell asleep feeling pushed by the Holy Ghost to come out to my ward the next morning. I woke up at 2 a.m. still being nagged. I prayed and went back to sleep. A couple of hours later, I woke up again with a strong presence in my bedroom. *Seriously? This is getting a little tiring.*

I popped awake yet again about five minutes before my alarm went off. When I picked up my phone, I bumped the play button on a podcast I'd been listening to the night before.

"Welcome to the podcast *Listen, Learn, and Love,* hosted by Richard Ostler. This initial podcast is an introduction podcast, so you will know the later content that you will potentially be listening to."

The *Listen, Learn, and Love* podcast is created by a member of the Church who is an LGBT ally. Richard specifically states that he has no intention of trying to change Church doctrines or policies but is seeking to create a more welcoming environment within the Church family for our LGBT brothers and sisters. He formed a non-profit organization and began the podcast when he heard the news of a gay teenager's suicide due to his sexual orientation. The announcement affected Richard deeply, and he was determined to help make a change in the Church's culture.

I can take a hint, even though this was well past a hint. More like a kick in the head. I still didn't feel comfortable about announcing my sexual orientation in sacrament meeting, so I went to church praying that plenty of other people would be prompted to share their own testimonies and use up the allotted time. If only.

When I entered the chapel, I met a friend I hadn't seen in a while. A few months prior, she had shared with me that she was struggling with her faith and testimony and felt that she was letting down her gay friends by belonging to the LDS Church. I sat with her through the sacrament and the bishopric introduction to open the pulpit for testimonies.

No one moved. After a couple of minutes, I thought, *Okay, God, I get it.* But before I could stand, someone else finally advanced to the rostrum, only to give accolades to me and a couple of other people for helping her through a rough time. I was self-conscious about the praise but hoped that this would get the meeting moving.

Nope! Another period of quiet. *All right, God, you don't have to tell me twice.* I made my way to the podium, shaking like I was going through a caffeine withdrawal. I had no idea what was going to come rolling out of my mouth.

I commented that I was the least likely person that you would see joining the Church. I had spoken recently to Richard from the *Listen, Learn, and Love* podcast—he has become a personal friend. He and I have talked about me wanting to push a button or take a pill to change myself. I eventually came to accept myself as I am, and that's gay. He's helped me to see that if I were to push a button or take a pill to change my sexual orientation, I would wipe out my entire existence. I don't want to do that.

Richard is a former young-adult ward bishop in Salt Lake City, and when he started his podcast, he was flooded with requests to speak to him. When anyone came out to him as gay, he did not take away their temple recommend. He did the opposite—he encouraged them to attend the temple even more often so they could feel the love of God in their hearts. We're all children of God. Christ chose to spend His time with lepers, the crippled, and people who weren't understood or were different. He listened to them, and He loved them.

I've had my own moments of being judgmental—I used to be very critical of smokers until the stake president told me straight out, "We need to smell more smoke in our church." He meant that we need to include people regardless of their actions. If we smell smoke in our chapels, it means that a smoker is attending church! They're trying to improve their lives! We need to support that!

I surprised precisely no one with my statement of being gay. But I felt more at one with myself and the ward knowing it was out in the open with no question. This was pivotal.

After sacrament meeting, I was greeted by so many ward members thanking me for my courage, confiding about various family members who are gay, and even saying, "Man, I never could have done what you just did!" The friend I was sitting with for the day was especially touched and said that my words helped to strengthen her faith.

I was pulled aside by one of the bishopric members, asking if I had a moment to talk. *Oh boy, here it comes. I've done it now. This is because I just came out as an openly gay Mormon.*

I really need to give these people more credit and stop panicking every time one of the leaders wants to talk to me. He didn't say a word about sacrament meeting. He asked me to accept a calling to be a ward missionary.

"Oh my, well, um, YES! I would love that!" I had no idea at first what that entailed, but I already worked regularly with the local missionaries. Now I would be doing it in an official capacity.

On the flip side, I was still not out as a Mormon to most of my family and friends. I had not "come out" on social media or announced my baptism in a public way. I posted occasional pictures of myself with missionaries or in front of the temple, but didn't say exactly who I was with or where I was. Most people didn't think twice about it—I've always posted lots of photos with many, many different people. For the most part, my friends felt I was too gay or too smart to ever become Mormon.

But sometimes I'm not the brightest bulb on the Christmas tree. It was becoming apparent in social media that I didn't "just happen" to keep running into Mormon missionaries everywhere I went. People were wondering and started bringing it up.

When I hesitantly shared my conversion story and told friends that I had been baptized, they were floored. I was bombarded with alarming warnings.

"Are you nuts? What were you thinking?" They reminded me again and again that Mormons are the largest haters of gays. They would put me through conversion therapy. They wanted me to get married to a Mormon woman and start having children. My father even said once that he was concerned I'd come home with multiple husbands. Gosh, for thirty years, I couldn't find even one husband, and now they're worried about multiple husbands?

A major shift was occurring in my life as my friends perceived changes in my lifestyle: I toned down my vocabulary, my behavior was not as risqué, I declined a glass of wine, and a gap was growing. I noticed that I was being invited to fewer events, parties, and social gatherings by my LGBT friends. Even my straight friends were becoming more distant. Who's left from my pre-Mormon life? Well, one staple in my life is my darling and precious little dog, Miss Pickles.

Now that it's been over a year, I think my family realizes that this is not a phase I'm going through. I've made a commitment to God that I intend to keep for the rest of my life.

Just like Al Carraway doesn't want to be labeled as the tattooed Mormon, I don't want to be labeled as the gay Mormon. I'm just Dennis, who happens to be gay and happens to be Mormon all at the same time. Why must we spend so much time and energy labeling, judging, and criticizing people for not living exactly as we do? We're all unique! Let's turn up the love and accept people as they are. As my friend Richard teaches, "Listen, learn, and love."

I've always had a mantra: Treat others the way you expect to be treated. Don't let negative comments from anyone bring you down. Look for the good in all creation.

As I ponder my journey, I'm reminded that we all have agency. Agency is the ability to make decisions, to choose between right and wrong. I may not have always chosen the correct path, but it later seems to reveal itself. And trust me, when you choose the right and do good, great things will happen to you in return. You can call them gifts, blessings, or just plain luck. Personally, I consider them blessings from Heavenly Father.

This has become my new emotional security.

There is nothing in the gospel of Jesus Christ that is homophobic or that would lend itself to anti-gay action or rhetoric, so we should be ever watchful against allowing such prejudices to seep into our culture and discourse. Moreover, the Church teaches that all human beings are created in the image of God, we are the beloved spirit sons and daughters of Heavenly Parents, and everyone has a divine nature and destiny (see "The Family: A Proclamation to the World"). We have immense potential to be pure Christians—and LGBT allies—by treating all of God's children with the dignity, honor, love, and friendship that we all deserve by divine birthright.

I challenge you to do good, and I promise that phenomenal things will occur within your life. God "delights to honor those who serve [him] in righteousness and truth" throughout our lives (D&C 76:5).

Chapter 14

Temple Time

At the temple the dust of distraction seems to settle out,
the fog and the haze seem to lift, and we can "see" things
that we were not able to see before and find a way through
our troubles that we had not previously known.[9]

~ Boyd K. Packer

My temple preparation class at church was unusually large. A number of us, converts and youth getting ready to serve missions, were preparing at the same time to go through the temple. Before I only had a limited temple recommend card, now I was receiving the blessings to have a full temple recommend allowing me to perform sacred ordinances.

I had gone to the temple multiple times to perform proxy baptisms, and I was eager to be allowed to participate in the rest of the temple ceremonies. We fed off each other's enthusiasm for this important step in our faith.

Converts can go to the temple when they've been a member for a year, and I took that very literally. The first anniversary of my baptism landed on a Sunday, so I was asked to go the day before because the temples are not open on Sundays.

I called Andrew and Audrey to let them know the date I'd selected, and they were so disappointed that they wouldn't be able to come to the East Coast for the occasion. Andrew had a mandatory orientation for graduate school the same weekend.

At first, I was fine. "Don't worry about it! It will all work out!" But when I got off the phone, doubt and nervousness set in and I had a brief conversation with Lucifer. I immediately recognized the problem signs and prayed.

"Heavenly Father, I ask you to surround me with the presence of the Holy Ghost to protect me from evil. Please keep it away and surround me with your glorious presence."

A sense of peace enveloped my body.

When I called the temple to schedule my appointment, I had a wonderful chat with the secretary. She said she'd been expecting me and even already knew how to spell my last name, even though we'd never met. Surprisingly, I didn't find that weird at all. I guess I have quite the reputation in the Church already—I hope that's a good thing.

She asked for all my information—date of birth, date of baptism, recommend ID number, home and email address, my parents' names, and on and on. I felt like I was applying for a mortgage.

But a red flag popped up. Apparently, the one-year mark from baptism is a hard line and if you precede it by even one day—as I was requesting—the temple computer system raises an alert that there's extra paperwork for the stake president to file.

When I talked to the stake president about it, he asked that since he was filing the paperwork anyway, was there a specific date significant to me? Well, my birthday was the week before my baptism, and on a Saturday that year. But after that, I told the stake president that if he felt otherwise, I was willing to wait one month, two months, even a year or more. He looked me in the eyes and assured me that there was no problem with moving forward as planned. "You've worked hard. You've dedicated your life to the Church. You deserve this." Then that was the date for the paperwork, and a week later, we had the green light.

I was elated to have this amazing way to celebrate my birthday and texted many of my LDS friends to let them to know block it into their calendars. Even if they couldn't come to Connecticut, I hoped they would partake in my temple day by serving in their local temples at the same time I was participating in the ceremonies for the first time.

I was over my fear of being called into the bishop's office by then, so I was cheerful when his secretary pulled me out of a Sunday class to have my official temple recommend interview. My bishop is amazing! From day one, he has always been supportive and full of light. He has a constant smile and is a joy to speak with.

The stake president is no different from the bishop. Both carry and disseminate the love of God to others so completely that when you're with them, you have no question that Jesus Christ loves you and that these men are His servants to help you feel that love.

To fit me into his busy schedule, I had to go to the stake president's house for my second interview, up on a mountain with an amazing view of rolling hills and beautiful green trees. I met his wife, and we chatted for a bit before proceeding into his office for my formal interview.

The stake president loves to talk and share stories, as do I obviously, and this went on for literally hours. We discussed this book project, which was already underway, his feeling that there is a tremendous gap between LGBT people and the culture of the Latter-day Saint community, and goals to overcome that gap.

The official interview went in stops and starts throughout our exchange, but I was running out of energy. "I don't mean to be rude, but it's getting late."

He frowned, kidding. "What? Are you not enjoying our conversation?"

"Of course I am. It's just, well . . ." I stopped and then blurted it out. "It's fast Sunday, and I haven't been home to eat yet."

"Oh, I'm so sorry! Do you like steak?"

This was absolutely hilarious to me. My favorite part of Al Carraway's book is that she originally told the missionaries she would only listen to their message about the gospel if they brought her a steak. They did, later that day. Now I had a steak dinner in common with her.

The stake president headed into his kitchen and removed the food from the refrigerator. A steak was plunked onto a paper plate, mashed potatoes, and gravy poured over it, salad dumped on top of that, and a paper towel placed over the whole thing so I could get it home to reheat.

Best dinner ever.

Late that night, I got a phone call from Andrew. He told me that he and Audrey had just had dinner with his sister, Amy, and asked if I was sitting down. Umm, okay. "Amy is going to use her frequent flyer miles to get me a plane ticket to Hartford for your temple session. I'll be landing in New Jersey Thursday night."

My heart felt like it was going to burst with explosive happiness. I was laughing and crying and shaking all at the same time. Andrew hadn't been able to attend my baptism in person, but now he could be my assisting guide at the temple because I had changed the date to my birthday and through the generosity of his sister! I was so overjoyed that I could barely contain myself. There is definitely a Higher Power that allowed for these circumstances to occur.

Andrew laughed delightedly. "If I knew you were going to be *that* excited, I would have recorded it!"

The next four days were the longest of my life, much more than the days between my return from Palmyra, New York, and when I attended church for the first time. I had set myself up though. That previous Sunday, the day of my stake president interview and Andrew's call, I had shared in testimony meeting that I was experiencing no set-backs, roadblocks, or challenges. I even went so far as to say, "When are these blessings going to stop?"

Wednesday. Roadblock Wednesday.

I was on my way to the temple shop to purchase the white clothing that is always worn inside the temples. I needed to stop by my parents' home on my way to arrange for me to take care of some things for them while they were on a vacation. In conversation with my mother, I told her about the blessing of Andrew coming to town for my birth-day, and he would be with me the next time I came to the house.

My mother leveled my spirit with a daunting glare. "Absolutely not! He is definitely not welcome here. He's evil! Your father and the other deacons in our church prayed, and we consider your church to be the work of Satan!"

This was a giant blow, and I felt like all the oxygen had been force-fully sucked out of my lungs. Without thinking, I looked into her eyes. "Mom, you're the devil!"

I stormed out and went on my way to the distribution center, but here came the black cloud of loneliness and insecurity. *I don't deserve this. How can I go through the temple when I just called my mother the devil?*

I pulled into the parking lot only to discover that it had closed ten minutes earlier. Defeat. I collapsed against the car's steering wheel. Downward emotional spiral. *This is a sign that I shouldn't go to the temple.* But a tiny part of my spirit wasn't letting go, and I remembered my buddy system, like Paula had talked about at my baptism. The buddy system isn't just spiritual with the Holy Ghost. It's also people.

Shelby is so reliable. She answered the phone immediately and consoled me as well as anyone can from two thousand miles away. "I'm so proud of you for preparing to go to the temple. Remember that life is always a test. Satan is not done with you yet. In fact, he will never been done with any of us. All I can say is to pray, read the scriptures, and keep an open mind because the gospel of Jesus Christ is true. I know what you are about to do is the right next step. I will be there with you in spirit and holding your hand all the way."

I felt the tension and self-deprecation leave my body each time I exhaled, with her soothing voice in my ear. She also reminded me that I would be further protected spiritually when Andrew landed on the East Coast the next night. He would be a real-life guardian angel.

"I need my angel fast, like now. Can't he be teleported here?"

I stayed busy all day Thursday to distract myself, until it was time to leave for the airport. I got a haircut, I went to the distribution center when it was *open* to get my temple clothes, and I made arrangements for Andrew to stay at the home of a member of my ward. I have my own rules and standards about being with men, and I was not comfortable with Andrew staying in my home without his wife. I don't ever want things to be misunderstood or misinterpreted, especially not relating to straight allies to the LGBT community.

When Andrew texted that his plane was on the ground, I was flooded with an overwhelming sensation that everything was fine now. My guardian angel had arrived safely. I hadn't seen him for about ten months, since my trip to Utah the previous October. We picked up right where we left off, as if the verbal conversation had never stopped in all that time.

My temple visit was on Saturday, so we had all day Friday to ourselves. He had only visited New England for work, so he only knew the airport, major interstates, hotels, and convention centers. I wanted him to have a true New England experience and had a list of places to go.

Just before getting in my car, I noticed there was a car behind mine. I thought, *I can just move around, no big deal.* Seconds later, I put the car in reverse, slammed on the gas—*CRASH!*

I sideswiped the entire side of this stranger's car. *Dang it, are you kidding me? I'm supposed to be protected from the adversary now!* But obviously not from other vehicles. I got out of my car to check out the damage, and dropped to my knees on the pavement in hysterics.

When I finally got to Andrew, I just handed him my keys. "You're driving." Before we went anywhere, he gave me a priesthood blessing of comfort, which allowed my spirit to return to earth.

We visited a friend who secured the back bumper on my car with duct tape, since I didn't want to lose time taking it to a mechanic. Vicki and Donnie were delighted to have us over and talk. It was nice to have friends from two different sectors of my life connect with each other. It was an interesting conversation between a Mormon and a former Jehovah's Witness. They exchanged information about the different beliefs and were able to find common ground.

We visited a beautiful state park with a "castle"—an elaborate home built by a wealthy actor who died with no heirs, so the state ended up with the property. I knew Andrew would love all the magical photo opportunities of the castle, the trails, and the awe-inspiring view of the Connecticut River.

We also went up to Springfield, Massachusetts, to the national Basketball Hall of Fame. Andrew is a basketball enthusiast and had always wanted to go there. No one would go with him but a true friend—not even his wife would have gone. I'd never been there even though it's close. I don't know the first thing about sports and always confuse terms. I knew it would bring him joy and I wanted him to have a good time, so we went. Yep, I made a fool out of myself attempting to throw balls into the hoop. Isn't that what life is all about? Shouldn't you be able to laugh at yourself?

Then the challenge. I still needed to go to my parents' house, but I was with Andrew, whom my mother had forbidden from being there. We went anyway.

We started next door at my grandmother's house. I wanted to introduce Andrew to this woman who has had great influence in my life, who has provided me with wisdom, who always has my back. She has never judged me or called down the wrath of God on me. My ninety-five-year-old grandmother is to be treasured as much as my brother. Andrew loved meeting her. She shared stories from my childhood, and I asked her if I could show him the basement where we used to have our massive feasts for holidays and celebrations.

While we were in the basement, I received a text from my father. "Where are you? I still need to show you how to operate the John Deere."

Really? I've been mowing that lawn since I was a child. I was forty-six, and there was nothing about that machine he could show me that I didn't already know. I think it was his way of indicating that it would be all right to take Andrew over to their house. I was still nervous, but the Holy Ghost gave me a calming feeling that everything would be fine.

We strolled across the yard, and I introduced Andrew to my father. My dad was warm and welcoming. My mother had been inside packing for their vacation but came out and also introduced herself. I took care of the vacation arrangements, and Andrew reminded me of the perfect missionary. He asked polite questions and said how much he, his parents, and his wife all respect and value their son. As we were leaving, Andrew asked if we could all take a picture together.

I flinched. *Oh heavens, this is not good. My parents probably think I'm going to post this on Facebook. They can't stand social media.*

Shockingly, they perked right up. "Oh sure, let's get a picture!"

What the heck was that? Kudos to my parents—they were the perfect hosts. There was nothing negative, religious, or argumentative. You'd never know that two days earlier, they'd forbidden Andrew from stepping foot onto their property. I'm not sure if it was just a front. I was hoping in my heart of hearts there was more to it, that they genuinely liked Andrew.

I was awake and up early on my forty-sixth birthday. It was going to be the best day ever, going through the temple with Andrew and many friends from church. Andrew was there specifically to be my teacher. When you receive your first ordinances in the temple, you choose

Dennis with his parents, Andrew, and Miss Pickles

someone to be your guide to answer questions, help you through the process, and make sure you don't get lost.

In the early morning light, I prayed and reflected on what was coming. I made some notes in my diary:

> This is your day. Try to relax and enjoy it. Don't forget to look around the room several times to notice all the people who are there for you today.
>
> Leave your phone, watch, and any distractions in your car.
>
> This is sacred time. Keep it private between you and the Lord, and share sparingly only if prompted by the Holy Ghost.
>
> Bring honor to your ancestry by continuing to do temple work.
>
> Dive into Church history, the pioneers, Joseph Smith, revelations, etc. Learn their stories.

I met Andrew several hours before our temple appointment in the afternoon so that we could talk and he could give me any last minute preparation. He drove to the temple—I wasn't taking any chances with another car crash.

As we entered the temple, I was shaking and nervously handed my paperwork to the worker at the front desk. Andrew kept saying, "It's going to be okay. Just breathe."

Many people from my ward attended the temple with me. Some people traveled to be there, including my colleague Cheryl from Rhode Island, who had been the first person to ever confirm to me that she is a Latter-day Saint.

I hate to choose favorites, but it was so significant that Sister Esplin received permission to travel from over two hours away to be there for my temple session. She and I had connected so well while she and Sister Tumlinson were teaching me the lessons the year before. I wish Sister Tumlinson could have been there with us too, but she had already completed her mission assignment and gone home to California.

I'll not go into details about my private time in the temple as I am heeding the advice to keep it sacred and personal. The only thing I will say is that I felt as if I floated through the entire experience. The same as at my baptism, I looked around to notice all the people who were there for me. After the ordinances, we entered the celestial room together. It's a room that is representative of heaven and being in the presence of God with our families and friends. To me, it *was* heaven and I *was* in the presence of God with my family and friends.

As Andrew and I wrapped up our day where he was staying, he whipped out a bag, pulled it open, and started handing me cards and gifts. I was shocked—just having him there had been more than enough. Andrew recorded me with his phone as I opened the presents from his wife, in-laws, and parents. When I got to the last card, a wad of cash fell out of the envelope. I was beyond emotional at this point. I had such a hard time grasping that these people who I had met only once were giving me cash. I have truly been included in their family circle.

Andrew and I were able to spend two more days together. We attended church together for the first time, with me wearing socks that say "Fishers of Men" on the soles—a reference to Peter in the Bible. I was asked to make an impromptu statement during sacrament meeting. I, of course, had nothing prepared. I prayed for guidance from the Holy Ghost to provide a message that would share conviction, honesty, and strength. He did not let me down.

That evening, we visited two different families in the ward that evening who Andrew had heard a lot about from me over the past year, and I was so grateful that my Connecticut friends and family were starting to blend with my Utah friends and family.

Monday morning—New York City, here we come! Let the fun begin! (As if it had ever stopped!) I still wasn't leaving anything to chance. As soon as I picked up Andrew, I handed him my car keys. I didn't even care that he's only in his twenties, a baby in my eyes. I felt safer with him driving.

We went all over the city for the entire day. It's Andrew's favorite place on the entire planet. Sadly, we had to end our excursion at the airport so he could go home to Audrey. I wish he didn't have to go, but I knew he missed his sweet wife. I was stuck driving myself again with him gone, but the drive was peaceful as the Tabernacle Choir as I went back to Connecticut.

Chapter 15

Why I Believe

Love is the greatest of all the commandments—all others hang
upon it. It is our focus as followers of the living Christ. It is
the one trait that, if developed, will most improve our lives.[10]

~ Joseph B. Wirthlin

In some of my travels, I attended a ward in Myrtle Beach, South
Carolina, and met a beautiful family visiting from Virginia that shared
a heart-wrenching story.

They had lost their bishop just the week before from their home
ward when his young teenage son came out of the closet as gay. The
bishop and his wife decided to leave the church that I hold near and
dear to my heart. They took their five children with them because
they were afraid their son would not be accepted within the Latter-day
Saint world. I have a message for that family and many others who feel
the same.

I've personally visited many wards all over the United States and
encountered nothing but love, understanding, and open arms. I can't
express enough the happiness and joy I've experienced as I share with
new people that I am a gay convert to The Church of Jesus Christ of
Latter-day Saints. I receive a hand on my shoulder, hugs from heterosexual men, and tears from women expressing their encouragement.

Many people tell me that they have a gay friend who is a member of the Church, though most of the time not actively attending or participating in their ward and the gospel.

It is sadly true that there will be people who are not as accepting as the many I've met in my journey. I have spoken to a number of parents whose teenage and young adult children are questioning whether they will remain active and engaged in the gospel. It is heartbreaking for me to hear what is being said to them or about them in Church culture. My goal in writing this book is to offer further education that will lead to better understanding of the many beautiful LGBT brothers and sisters in the world, both in and out of our church.

Every morning in prayer, I say that this book, though it is my story, is not about me. It is about you, the one who is reading this. And in a way, I am still that seventeen-year-old boy going on national TV. If sharing my story will help one person know that they are not alone, then it is worth it to me. I pray every day that this story can help those in need of it.

I know many of my non-LDS gay friends can relate to being victimized because of our sexual orientation. I know women who have been discriminated against in the workplace or out in public. I know African Americans who have it tough because they're viewed as different. I also know our Heavenly Father created all men and women equal and loves each and every one of us. That's why I say, let's turn up our love for all. We need more people sharing love and kindness. I try to lead by example, sharing love by doing small random acts of kindness.

If you have been part of somebody's pain by participating in hateful comments, please repent. People who are different don't need to be criticized, ridiculed, judged, or mocked. Sexual orientation is not a fault or a choice. If you don't understand, try to. Listen, support, and love. In the world we live in and share, no matter what religion or orientation we are, we all just need to share more love.

Since I've been baptized, a number of positive things have occurred within the Church. One of the most substantial ones to me is that when the Tabernacle Choir toured California in June 2018, the San Francisco Gay Men's Chorus was invited to perform with them and their artistic director was the guest conductor. The Church also donated $25,000 to suicide prevention training.

I am thrilled to see these steps. I must be clear that I did not join the Church to change policies or views about LGBT issues, but it does bring great joy when our LGBT brothers and sisters are more openly included and accepted than they were in the past.

I've received validation that love for LGBTs is spreading at an individual level as well. I recently received a photo from one of the sister missionaries who I had the pleasure of teaching many discussions with. She was released a few months ago and sent me a photo taken at general conference with Peter, who's gay and LDS. He started an awareness project of going to general conference and holding colorful signs outside the Conference Center saying, "Hug a Gay Mormon!" My former missionary was so excited to meet him in Utah and share the photo with me. She had previously confessed that she didn't know any gay people at all before she met me, and her impressions of LGBTs have broadened considerably since then.

I can honestly say that The Church of Jesus Christ of Latter-day Saints is by far the safest church I've ever attended. It's imperative for everyone to know that God loves you, no matter your race, sexual orientation, financial background, or anything else. It was this knowledge that God loves me, with the continuing confirmation from the Holy Ghost, that brought me into this church.

I also believe in my heart through my own personal revelation, that this Church is by far the most accepting of LGBT members, *based on what I've experienced*. This may not be the case for past members or people who left the Church. Other churches have also experienced hate crimes because of a lack of understanding and tolerance for people's differences. That was a different era and times are changing. We are a church of prophecy and revelation.

I understand that a lot of people may not comprehend or approve of me being gay and a worthy temple recommend holder of The Church of Jesus Christ of Latter-day Saints. Furthermore, I know that a lot of my gay friends will never understand why I became a Latter-day Saint and will distance themselves from me. It's okay! I still love and care deeply for everyone! That's the difference between someone who is striving to be a true disciple of Jesus Christ and someone who needs to do a little more work loving and accepting those they may not understand. I'm writing this at the risk of losing friendships and work relationships and upsetting my family for divulging my innermost secrets and struggles. Nothing can change this if it needs to be done.

We all have agency, the ability to choose what direction to go when faced with a challenging situation. I choose to go right—CTR. I choose to follow the commandments, the Word of Wisdom, and the restored gospel. You have agency as well, the personal autonomy to make correct decisions in your own life and journey on this earth that I believe in my heart will lead to eternal life.

The past two years have been an emotional roller coaster. Definitely worth the ride. Sometimes to receive greater happiness in life, we need to experience the downs in order to appreciate the good times. I'm now closer to God than ever before.

What means the most to me are the letters I receive from people of all walks of life, thanking me for being true to who I am. They know they are not the only ones struggling, and they share love and kindness to uplift and support me in my own path.

Lay your burden at the Savior's feet. Let go of judgment. Allow Christ's Atonement to change and heal your heart. Love one another. Forgive one another. The merciful will obtain mercy.[11]

~ Dieter F. Uchtdorf

Chapter 16

Walking in Sunlight

That which is of God is light; and he that receiveth light,
and continueth in God, receiveth more light; and that
light groweth brighter and brighter until the perfect day.

~ Doctrine and Covenants 50:24

I use the phrase "falling upward" often. When people have a downward spiral in their lives, they often have to hit rock bottom before they turn to religion and can experience tremendous growth through faith. It's unfortunate that it takes someone experiencing a crash before they turn to the Lord and can receive many blessings from joining a church.

I know how that works because, as you've just read, that's exactly what happened to me. I'm now falling upward on the path of righteousness leading into the plan of salvation. I'm not saying that there are no hiccups along the way. No one is perfect, and we all have to strive to attain a place in life filled with peace.

We can gain peace in our hearts and minds no matter what is happening around us when we reach beyond our personal comfort zones to share love and kindness. For example, today, right now, think of how you can be of service by calling an old friend or someone you've not seen in some time. When you're in a challenging time, think of what our Savior would do. He was always serving others, even when He was tired or sad or just wanted to be alone for a while. Take a break from your troubles by focusing on others and helping with their lives.

It may have appeared that I experienced a lot of trials and tribulations throughout my journey becoming a member of The Church of Jesus Christ. Was it worth it? Absolutely!

What lessons did I learn from those trials? I learned that I must continue to have faith and trust in our Heavenly Father and trust in our Church leadership. The adversary is real, and through faith and prayer we can overcome any obstacle he may throw in our path.

Would I change anything during those turbulent moments? Yes, there is one thing. I wish I had realized sooner that developing a buddy system is crucial so you don't have to break through those stumbling blocks alone. There's a whole network of others who can help us bear our burdens.

> And it came to pass that he said unto them: Behold, here are the waters of Mormon (for thus were they called) and now, as ye are desirous to come into the fold of God, and to be called his people, and are willing to bear one another's burdens, that they may be light;
>
> Yea, and are willing to mourn with those that mourn; yea, and comfort those that stand in need of comfort, and to stand as witnesses of God at all times and in all things and in all places. (Mosiah 18:8–9)

These verses mean that we will be willing to bear one another's burdens and comfort each other in times of need. We will be there for all, no matter what race, religion, sexual orientation, gender, or disability.

We are all unique children of God on our own individualized journeys. Don't ever let another person's opinion of you define your self-worth. What anyone else thinks is irrelevant. The Lord's opinion is the one that matters, and He thinks the world of you.

Elder J. Devn Cornish of the Seventy made this statement in the October 2016 General Conference:

> Please, my beloved brothers and sisters, we must stop comparing ourselves to others. We torture ourselves needlessly by competing

and comparing. We falsely judge our self-worth by the things we do or don't have and by the opinions of others. If we must compare, let us compare how we were in the past to how we are today—and even to how we want to be in the future. The only opinion of us that matters is what our Heavenly Father thinks of us. Please sincerely ask Him what He thinks of you. He will love and correct but never discourage us; that is Satan's trick.[12]

On what would have been Darin's forty-second birthday, I was in Myrtle Beach on the boardwalk with a friend. I could feel his presence and was having a conversation with him as if he was there. I could definitely sense his joy and happiness for the changed person I have become. This friend is not a member of our church but has been supportive of my decision to be baptized. That day, she could feel his presence as well.

"Your brother is making me feel the calmest I have been in years," she told me. "I can feel his strength lifting me up. This is needed now more than ever as I'm at the lowest point I've ever experienced. My life is unraveling, but your brother is giving me hope."

This was the first time I had felt true conviction from her about anything spiritual. I talked to her about calling on our Heavenly Father in prayer at any time. We can all have that same experience if we just ask for His guidance. It may not come as quickly as you expect—you have to be open to receiving answers in the Lord's time and maybe in subtle ways—but He will always answer.

On February 1, Andrew sent me a text asking if I saw Sister Tumlinson's post about her mother passing away.

This brought me to my knees, asking Heavenly Father to take away her pain. When I was finally able to read her post, I was filled with a mix of emotions. Pain for my friend, love for her, pain at my relationship with my parents, and love for them. That love is and perhaps always will be wrapped up in other things, harsh and hurtful things. But it is there.

Sister Tumlinson wrote:

Everyone thinks their parents will live forever. You never imagine the day you will be planning your mother's funeral. I'm 22 years old. I'm too young to be writing her eulogy. But in the early hours of this morning, my mom slipped away to be in a better place. I'll never be able to hug her again. Never hear her say, "I love you," in this life. Never argue with her about calling me by my least favorite nickname and have her respond, "But you'll always be my little Libis." But I'm glad she isn't in pain anymore and that her suffering is over. I know she'll be able to take care of us so much better as a spirit than she ever could from a hospital bed.

If I have learned one thing, it's to cherish your loved ones even if you don't always get along. Please tell your parents you love them. Spend time with your little siblings. Be a better friend. You never know when it could be the last time you tell someone you love them. So thank you, Mom, for teaching me all these things.

I replied to her post:

Sister Tumlinson,
Your post is so well written. Remember what you and Sister Esplin taught me, the veil is so thin. You can call on your mother anytime just as I do with my younger brother Darin. You are LOVED . . . Please text me your address.
Love, Dennis

If there is one thing that I have learned, it is that life is very rarely neat and tidy. It does not go as we plan. Sometimes we make mistakes that take years to come back from. But none of that really matters if we do come back, if we do follow the Lord's plan. Life is supposed to be messy. And the Atonement of Jesus Christ is there for all who will come unto Christ.

As I have searched out the Lord, the truth did in fact set me free. The Holy Ghost does exist. I can be my true self as a member of the Lord's Church who is gay and will not run from my past. In fact, I can now embrace my identity more fully than ever before.

No matter your religion, faith background, sexual orientation, or race, I challenge you to choose *love!* Open your heart, and you'll open your mind. Loving and accepting *all* is a true Christlike attribute. If you don't understand someone, ask them! If you have a friend who is dealing with depression and you don't have the comprehension of that experience, ask them what it is like to be depressed. If you don't understand what it's like to be LGBT, ask a person what it's like to be that way. By listening instead of lecturing, you can gain knowledge and understanding, which will help you love them more.

If you come to me with the challenges of your own life, I will listen and learn and love you. We can be united together as we seek to follow the Lord's admonition to love one another. If you're gay and don't want to leave the Church, you are not alone. Your struggle is my struggle. If you are gay and no longer Mormon, you're still my sister or brother. If you are straight, gay Latter-day Saints like me exist.

I finally found the emotional security I sought for so many years. That security falls within my faith and belief in The Church of Jesus Christ of Latter-day Saints.

Once more, *let's turn up the love*, and don't forget to *just pray*. Don't ever forget that there is hope. The answer to anything you've ever wanted to know, understand, or achieve is just a prayer away.

With much love and hugs to all,
Dennis Schleicher
#TurnUpTheLove

Resources

LDS Hotline

Call 1-888-537-6600 to speak directly with a missionary, or go online at www.mormon.org/chat to message with a missionary. Someone is available for your questions 24 hours a day.

Listen, Learn, and Love

The *Listen, Learn, and Love* podcasts by Richard Ostler share stories of people who are at the crossroads of being Latter-day Saint and LGBT. We invite everyone to follow the teachings of the Restored Church of Jesus Christ, and we support and affirm the individual decisions of each LGBT person without judgment. We leave judgment to our Savior and His perfect understanding. Listen to these stories at www.listenlearnandlove.org/podcasts.

Communities

LGBT National Hotline (1-888-843-4564): offers peer counseling, information, and local resources

National Runaway Safeline (1-800-RUN-AWAY or 1-800-786-2929; www.1800runaway.org)

Suggested Books

That We May Be One: A Gay Mormon's Perspective on Faith and Family by Tom Christofferson

More than the Tattooed Mormon, Second Edition by Al Carraway

References

1. Ellen DeGeneres as quoted in David Hochman, "Ellen DeGeneres: Nice Girls Finish First," *Good Housekeeping*, September 10, 2011, https://www.goodhousekeeping.com/life/inspirational-stories/interviews/a18893/ellen-degeneres-interview.
2. Barbara Bush, in a letter to Paulette Goodman, 1990, as quoted in "Our Story," *PFLAG*, https://pflag.org/our-story.
3. "Closing Epilogue," *Les Misérables*, music and lyrics by Claude-Michel Schönberg and Herbert Kretzmer (1986), based on the novel by Victor Hugo (1862).
4. Oprah Winfrey as quoted in Janet Lowe, *Oprah Winfrey Speaks: Insight from the World's Most Influential Voice* (Wiley, 1998), 169.
5. Dieter F. Uchtdorf, "O How Great the Plan of Our God!" *Ensign*, November 2016.
6. Dieter F. Uchtdorf, "Our True Identity," LDS Media Library, https://www.lds.org/media-library/video/2010-04-20-our-true-identity.
7. Bette Midler, *Saturday Review*, 1983.
8. Eleanor Roosevelt, *You Learn by Living: Eleven Keys for a More Fulfilling Life* (Harper, 1960), 29.
9. Boyd K. Packer, "The Holy Temple," *Ensign*, February 1995.
10. Joseph B. Wirthlin, "The Great Commandment," *Ensign*, November 2007.
11. Dieter F. Uchtdorf, "The Merciful Obtain Mercy," *Ensign*, May 2012.
12. J. Devn Cornish, "Am I Good Enough? Will I Make It?" *Ensign*, November 2016.

Acknowledgments

The entire staff at Cedar Fort: They broke the ground and made history along with providing countless hours of personal counseling when I was feeling hesitation in publishing this book—along with everyone who played a part in this transformative memoir and life journey.

My literary agent, Gina Panettieri: She has provided countless hours of "therapy," listening to my struggles and concerns with this project from the beginning.

My entire ward and stake, and every Latter-day Saint congregation I've visited while traveling around our beautiful country: I've been welcomed everywhere with open arms as a gay convert.

All of the missionaries: I can't tell you how many have allowed me to help spread the gospel through teaching with them.

John Trau: Without knowing me other than through Facebook, he met me for dinner while I was traveling and shared his conversion story as an openly gay convert over thirty years ago. It reassured me I'd made the right decision in my own life.

Derek and Shelby Hall, Devin Glazier, Craig Johanson, and their entire families: You always respected me and never judged me. Your examples led me to listen, to learn, to love, and to become more Christlike.

Andrew and Audrey Earl and their entire family (Doug, Lisa, Brian, Judy, Amy, Jenna, Ryan, and Blake): You've allowed me to be part of your family and claimed me as your own. You've touched my heart with so many blessings and played a major role in shaping who I am today.

And to everyone else who has helped, strengthened, and supported me on my journey in any way—I thank you from the bottom of my heart.

About the Author

Dennis Schleicher is a writer, lifestyle reporter, crisis counselor, network marketer, and motivational speaker. Dennis is vice president and publicity director of the Connecticut Authors & Publishers Association, has a degree in essential oils chemistry and pharmacology, and hosts the cable show "The Art of Aromatherapy."

Dennis currently works as a network marketer, helping others to achieve financial success through creating residual income. He has worked at several Fortune 500 companies, including working as a regional sales manager representing a multimillion-dollar territory within the professional beauty industry. It is through his work